Temperament Styles in Adult Interaction

Applications in Psychotherapy

Temperament Styles in Adult Interaction

Applications in Psychotherapy

by
JAYNE BURKS, Ph.D.
and
MELVIN RUBENSTEIN, M.D.

BRUNNER/MAZEL, *Publishers* • New York

Library of Congress Cataloging in Publication Data

Burks, Jayne, 1920-
    Temperament styles in adult interaction.

    Bibliography: p.
    Includes index.
    1. Psychotherapy.   2. Temperament.   3. Social interactions.   I. Ruben-
stein, Melvin, 1921-   joint author.   II. Title.
RC480.5.B798   616.8'914   79-52532
ISBN 0-87630-202-9

Published by
BRUNNER/MAZEL, INC.
19 Union Square
New York, New York 10003

Foreword

The past five years or so have witnessed a rapidly increasing number of studies of temperament, its relationship to other organismic and environmental factors, and its significance for healthy and deviant psychological functioning. This has taken place both in this country and in centers in many other countries. The interest in temperament has reflected several currents in recent developmental research and theory: 1) the accumulating evidence that an exclusively environmentalist and psychodynamic view is insufficient to explain individual differences in psychological development; 2) the weight of careful research studies documenting the active role in the parent-child interaction played by the child's own perceptual and behavioral characteristics from the moment of birth on; and 3) the resolution of the age-old argument over hereditary and constitution versus environment in biology and psychology in favor of the view that an individual's characteristics are always the product of a constantly evolving nature-nurture interactional process.

The interactional approach has been crucial in conceptualizing the role of temperament (as well as other influential factors) in the developmental process. Previous mechanistic views had counterposed biology to culture, and heredity-constitution to environment as antagonists operating in opposition, or at best independently of each other. From the beginning of our own New York Longitudinal Study almost 25 years ago, Dr. Stella Chess and I have challenged this mechanistic view, and insisted that any attribute of functional developmental significance—whether temperament, abilities, motivations or environmental opportunities and demands—cannot be considered in isolation, but only as one factor in a constantly evolving interactional process of all influential variables. This interactional concept (or transactional, as some prefer to call it) has also been increasingly emphasized in other major longitudinal studies, as the only theoretical framework that can do justice to the developmental research findings.

In this recent period, studies of temperament, including our own New York Longitudinal Study, have concentrated on the childhood period. This does not in any way mean that temperamental attributes are unimportant in shaping psychological individuality and patterns of behavior in the adult. Quite the contrary. In fact, it was our impressionistic identification of temperamental patterns in adults, as well as in the children we knew personally and professionally, and our judgment that these patterns had functional significance, that stimulated our original interest in studying this psychological attribute. However, the task of identifying and categorizing the separate elements of behavior—temperament, abilities and motivations —is highly complex in the adult as compared to the child. Behavioral repertoires are elaborate; cognitive and motivational patterns are highly conceptualized and symbolized. Temperament enters into complex interactional processes with these other attributes of the individual and with a host of environmental factors, and the identification of the stylistic component in any item or pattern of behavior becomes much more difficult than in the child.

The problem of identifying and rating temperament in the adult is further compounded by the increasing individual variations in activities of all kinds which emerge as children grow older. As a result, the standardization of protocols, questionnaires, scoring criteria and qualitative ratings for temperament becomes increasingly complex for the older child, adolescent, and adult.

Previous efforts by other investigators at categorizing and rating temperament in the adult have had limited usefulness. With few exception these approaches have ignored the necessity for an interactionist view of development, or have developed global and simplistic categories, or have failed to explore the place of temperament in the dynamics of psychological development and behavioral functioning. We ourselves are only now turning our attention to these issues as the subjects of the New York Longitudinal Study are entering early adult life.

Seen against this background, Drs. Burks and Rubenstein have undertaken an important, ambitious and pioneering task. Out of their extensive experience in psychotherapy and counseling, they have affirmed not only the possibility but the importance of a systematic identification of the temperamental traits of individual adult patients and clients. They have spelled out the approach required to apply their concepts of temperament to practical psychotherapeutic and counseling work. They have explored the pertinence of temperament for the broader psychological questions of self-identity and individuality, and placed the psychological issues within a broad sociological perspective. At the same time, Drs. Burks and Rubenstein make it clear at the outset of the first chapter that they "do not see temperament as the only, or even the most important, determinant of behavior." To make temperament the heart and body of a general theory would be to repeat a frequent approach in psychiatry which, over the years, has been beset by general theories of behavior based upon fragments rather than the totality of influencing mechanisms. To ignore the role of temperament, on the other hand, would require substitute formulations of hypothetical and elusive complex intrapsychic subjective states.

The authors have a clear commitment to an interactionist view which is consonant with current concepts in developmental psychology. Of necessity, however, their emphasis throughout is on the significance of temperament, inasmuch as their special contribution lies in this direction. As we have experienced in our own studies of temperament, Drs. Burks and Rubenstein have found that they have ventured into an area that "is booby-trapped with leftover land mines of past wars—the booby traps of constitutionality, of labeling, of determinism." Hopefully, their emphasis that temperament is not the only, or even the most important determinant of behavior, and that temperament is influential through its interaction with other psychological attributes, will meet the objective response that was not generally possible in the dominant one-sided environmentalist views of the 1950s.

The authors are struck, as we were originally, by the many dramatic vignettes of continuity of one or another specific temperamental trait from childhood into adult life. This question of continuity versus discontinuity over time is a basic issue for developmental theory currently, not only for temperament, but for all other psychological attributes and characteristics as well. Our own position is that development proceeds with both continuity and change enmeshed in a dialectical unity of opposites—what we have called a homeodynamic rather than a homeostatic view. This is in no way contradicts the authors' thesis that their therapeutic approach rests on the necessity of the acceptance of temperament as a primary base which the individual brings to the interaction with his environment. Where there is clear evidence of continuity of temperament from earlier life, it is easier for the patient to understand and accept this approach. But even if such evidence of continuity from the past is difficult or impossible to establish, the acceptance of one's temperament with dignity and self-respect is still a vital thesis. The individual may have to change certain nonadaptive behaviors and may have to consciously modify the expression of certain temperamental characteristics in certain situations if he is to achieve an optimal interactional relationship with the environment. But to do so on the basis of labeling his own temperamental individuality as pathological would be destructive to any constructive sense of positive self-identity. This fundamental thesis is affirmed and reaffirmed throughout this volume.

The delineation of a number of distinctive temperamental characteristics and clusters does not in any way mean that all of these attributes are equally important influences in every individual. One or several temperamental characteristics may be significant for the psychological development and functioning of one person while other attributes may be significant for another person, and so on. At one age period one temperamental cluster may be important for one or most individuals, and this may change at later ages. As a result, it is not enough to define the overall temperamental characteristics in any specific case; it is also necessary to identify the functionally significant attributes at that age period. The authors affirm independently from their work with adults our own experience in this regard. In fact, the same principle is applicable to the evaluation of personality traits. For any scheme of classification of personality types and characteristics, whether in the child or adult, the same variability of functional significance of specific traits is apparent from individual to individual, as is the case for temperament.

Perhaps the most original contribution of Drs. Burks and Rubenstein is their new concept of temperament as having certain dynamic consequences which have a motivational aspect. This goes beyond the formulation of the mutual interactional influence of temperament motivations and abilities on each other, and proposes that temperament may actually become motivational. The authors spell out this concept in detail with numerous clinical examples. This formulation raises a most intriguing theoretical question. Does the separation of behaviors into temperament, motivation and ability reflect the actual organization of psychological structure, or is it a convenient scheme for the study of different aspects of the same functional structure? The material presented in this volume offers much food for thought on this question.

Drs. Burks and Rubenstein have pursued their studies of temperament in the adult within the clinical qualitative framework. This is the approach which traditionally has led to so many vital hypotheses and discoveries in psychology, psychiatry and the medical sciences in general. As the authors recognize, their clinical data require verification, elaboration, modification and even significant changes through the application of appropriate quantitative methods. Within their clinical framework, other clinicians may also offer different interpretations for specific cases. But with the publication of this volume, the serious student of the dynamics of adult personality and the practitioner of psychotherapy and counseling now have a model and a springboard for the incorporation of concepts of temperament in their research and practical work.

ALEXANDER THOMAS, M.D.

Contents

Preface

INDIVIDUALITY IN COLLABORATION

When two people collaborate in writing a book, the way that they fit their individual styles of approaching the subject matter into a cohesive and comprehensive whole becomes the first order of business. Since this book is about the way that individual temperaments fit with other individual temperaments in social behavior, the review of our separate and individual progression toward this collaborative venture may be appropriate.

The courses and directions that our lives take are seldom chaotic and irrational. It often seems that a new idea stimulates, a new person in our lives inspires, or a new set of circumstances impels us, to move in new directions. However, in retrospect, we can trace the pathways in our lives which prepared us for accepting this stimulating idea, welcoming this inspiring interaction, and adjusting to these new circumstances. We think that the ways we have proceeded from different experiences in our adult lives to this present collaboration are expressions of the individuality of each of us.

* * * *

M.R.

In 1961, after a life of literary emptiness, I unexpectedly produced a paper titled, "A Purpose in Life." A short paper, I surprised myself with the concluding sentences, "So in the end, *purpose in life* is merely being oneself in life and not somebody else's self. Martin

Buber stated this concisely when discussing the core of Hasidism, 'Man cannot approach the divine by reaching beyond the human, he can approach Him through becoming human. To become human is what he, this individual Man, has been created for.' " This came after my first decade as a therapist—a decade in which I had involved myself with patients who were struggling with disappointment in themselves and the disappointment of others. They paraded their pain of alienation and non-acceptance of self. I sat and listened, and for a long time did not understand what they were saying to me. They were largely seen as the "misfits" of our world, much as I often felt myself the "misfit" fortunate enough to be in the psychiatrist's seat.

As I look back on this time, I recognize now that most of these people were coming to me apprehensively hopeful that I would recognize them. What do I mean by recognition? Simply that I would recognize and accept who they were—not who they hadn't become, not who they should be, not who they must be. So, I listened, but my dominant feeling continued to be that all of my patients were living a life of resistance. All we had to do was to remove the primary childhood conflicts and they would be free to fly. There was nothing we couldn't do, no role demand we could not accept, if we were but completely conflict-free to become these ideal selves. And there were boundless ideal selves to become—this was the era of the Common Person, our coming of age, our turn to thrust ourselves into the traditional American middle-class ideal of success, prosperity, happiness, and family fulfillment. My patients' complaints about themselves were thus met by me with increased expectations that they *could* become everything they "resisted" becoming, if only we could remove the primary conflict, reach the ultimate answer.

So about 11 years into my practice, this surprise paper came forth. I think it was jarred loose by a spate of young men and women who came crawling into therapy, beaten by life, wondering what their next step was going to be. I wish I could say I effected some special cure of them all, but I didn't. Perhaps most of them left strengthened for a short period of time, but eventually many succumbed to old clinging relationships where they continued their life of inadequacy. It took me some time to realize that there was nothing terribly wrong with these "kids." They simply were searching for the point where they could indentify and be themselves, but were caught in a dissonant demand to be somebody else's self. Heretofore, I had taken a therapeutic role that did not even deal with the actuality of self and determination of self-identification. I knew only that we were helpless victims of early trauma and nothing could be done till that was discovered and removed. I did not recognize that anyone could have any sense of *who* they were.

It was an achievement for me to finally realize that my patients did have a sense of who they were, but that this was mostly obscured by who they *weren't* being. When I finally accepted the idea, and need, of their being who they were, I then asked myself the question, "Who are they?" Much to my discomfort, no answer came to me. I struggled with this identity question with my patients for a number of years. I knew the answer lay in some basic concept of individuality. But what was this individuality? Was it just something I opted for impulsively, a kind of "leap of faith"? Was it learned? I kept looking for something that was basically the individual's—his to develop—not like anyone else's.

For the next seven to eight years, I kept searching for this dimension of individuality that eluded me. I was sympathetic with the struggle of young people in the 60s to "do their thing," "find their way." To a great degree, this led more to political action rather than to individual therapy. The high mark of this was the struggle against involvement in the Vietnam War. Although they found real satisfaction in this political action, it still seemed that a special dimension of individuality was missing.

Unknown to me, about ths same time, the New York Longitudinal Study, headed by Drs. Alexander Thomas and Stella Chess, now in its third decade, was underway. Thomas and Chess, through their work with parents and children, had begun to doubt some basic psychodynamic assumptions: 1) that the child is the complete victim of his parents; that whoever he or she is, is precisely because of the exquisite influence and molding of the parents; in other words, that the child comes into the world as a clean tablet to be written on; and 2) that a child's personality and behavior can be understood and explained by specific parent responses around various erogenous zones.

TEMPERAMENT STYLES IN ADULT INTERACTION

Thomas and Chess observed that children parented in the same way turned out differently. Symptomatic behaviors often did not reveal the history one would expect. As a result, they turned their attention toward the then somewhat discredited area of temperament. They set about drawing up their hypotheses that these dimensions could be identified, that they were there very early in life as a basic, given individual responsiveness and reactivity. That they were able to establish this is now 20-year-old history and can be confirmed in their publications.

While I was looking for the lost dimension in our individuality as adults, Chess and Thomas were going about recapturing the lost dimension of individuality in infants. Finally, in 1967, I was brought face to face with these facts when I was invited to review a book for the Journal of the Child Welfare League, *Temperament and Behavior Disorders in Childhood,* by Thomas, Chess, and Birch.

The work of Thomas and Chess immediately appealed to me. First, I foresaw the exciting possibility of a truly preventive psychiatric approach. Presuming the effects of dissonance as an essential part of the disturbing behavior of a child-parent relationship, we could now identify the temperament dimensions of all concerned and work toward a consonant fit. It would also seem plausible to think of later adult difficulties as related to chronic attempts to deal with and resolve the persistence of the dissonance, perhaps as maintained internally by the now grown-up adult. This might then be a source of further insight into problems of character formation and a developmental view that could hopefully avoid those early once-and-for-all reactive straitjackets.

Second, there was a revival of my inner conviction that we could become that individual we were meant to be. All my years as a therapist (and a patient) were bound up in the proposition that I was treating people in search of their authenticity. All too often their search had zeroed in to a retrospective examination of previous bits of childhood fantasies, hopeful that some initial place could be reached. From what I could see, search led into search, which led into search.

Not yet being certain of just how I wished to proceed to implement this concept, I turned my attention to the new humanistic therapies and spent a considerable amount of time being trained in Transactional Analysis. Although I found some value in understanding the idea of "Scripts" which were "imposed" on a child who "decided" to live according to these impositions, I again came away with the psychoanalytic view that we are only the outcome of our parents' responses to our instincts. The difference in Transactional Analysis was that now the child is responsible for having decided to take the "Script." There was the same intense search to remove "messages" of parental origin and to make decisions to change. Yet the "decision of change," despite the best intentions of the therapist, was usually along lines comprehensible and acceptable to the therapist. Often this meant much struggle by the patient to do something which seemed painfully inappropriate to him or her.

The enthusiasm I had for Thomas and Chess' work remained with me over the years after my review of their book. I often brought up the idea of given dimensions of temperament and, though my colleagues presented no intense objection to it, I experienced a strange response of non-recognition—as if people didn't know what to do with it. I found the work highly esteemed by those who had read it, but there was no encouragement to use it. Being strongly adaptive, I retreated from pushing the idea in the face of obvious resistance, but set its existence in my hidden, inner world, where I preserve my intuitive certainties, and waited for someone to do something about it.

* * * *

J.B.

About five years ago, my life turned in a new direction. It was not the first time, of course. For years I have been aware of new "passages" as I moved from one phase to a subsequent one. But in previous times, the experience had been, perhaps, less acutely felt. After the sudden death of my husband, whose emotional and physical condition had become heavy burdens for us both, I found myself experiencing a sense of freedom that I had almost lost touch with. The youngest of my four children was now in college. I had finally completed my Ph.D. and was teaching sociology in a small college. It was a time for me to think of new activities—a move to California? A new house? I was aware that I wanted to *do* something new.

In my new freedom and anticipation, friendships burgeoned, among them the one that has become so much a part of my life. I didn't move to California. I still live in the same house. We moved, rather, to professional collaboration and, eventually, to marriage.

We began a process that rehearsed for each other all the ideas that we had found stimulating and had yearned for someone else to recognize and respond to. It was a surprise to us, coming from totally different backgrounds and experiences, to discover that we shared points of view about so many things. Our present preoccupation with the importance of temperament in interaction seems to be, in fact, a continuation of a long-held interest for both of us.

For many years my interest in temperament was non-academic and non-professional. As a mother of four children, I was aware of the individuality of each child and of the differences in their ways of reacting. I was also aware of my own way of interacting with these children. Without such awareness, I would have been totally unprepared for the high contrast in style when my first child, who was relatively quiet and napped a lot, was followed by our second child, who remained awake, kicking and moving, from 7:00 a.m. to 7:00 p.m. when he was only weeks old, and managed to crawl out of his carriage at seven months. As if to emphasize the varieties of temperament, our third child expressed herself in great high spirits, torrential tears and an intensity that sometimes seemed overwhelming, while our fourth approached the world smilingly and trustingly (and found the world was sometimes not to be trusted).

The way that each of us relates to his or her surroundings is so apparent that it somehow has become "unremarkable," as if it has nothing to do with individual behavior. But in most families this individual temperamental style is at least a part of our interaction with each other. I can remember conversations with other parents like, "Ted hates it when he has to do something new. I will try to encourage him to come to Cub Scouts, but it generally takes him a while to get used to a new situation," or "Tommy gets involved in playing in his treehouse and won't stop for anything." These are statements that indicate we know how a person acts and that we take that knowledge into account. All of us, I suspect, are more or less aware of this identification of our "self" and recognize that others also have an individuality which underlies behavior. My further guess is that in those deeply satisfying friendships, truly intimate relationships, and really caring parent and child ties such recognition and acceptance of each other are the basis of the gratification that we feel.

But this sort of knowledge about children is not easily apparent to those who are not in daily and close contact with a child and the professionalization of child care seems to have emphasized quite different aspects of child behavior. Like most middle-class American mothers, I was eager to do the best I could for these children, and like most middle-class American mothers I looked to experts with their scientific knowledge of child-rearing for my guide. It has only been recently that I have begun to question the wisdom of this dependency upon professionals and of ignoring the more "intuitive" and private knowledge of children's lives in the family setting. It seemed that as parents we were trained by experts to think of our children as simply undifferentiated receivers of life experiences. As parents we bore the complete responsibility for the way they turned out. The most plaintive questions of parents are the well-worn, "Where did I go wrong? What should I have done?" I remember anxiously worrying to myself, "What am I doing to cause this outburst?" when my third child responded with cries of outrage when given a simple suggestion to wear her boots because it was raining! If I were only an effective parent, I should be able to properly motivate the child to do what was best for her (best in my eyes, of course). If I were really a "good mother," my children would all progress through life stages with excellent grades, many friends and physical agility, and be crowned in adult life with successful and richly rewarding marriages and careers.

To the worries of doing the right thing for my children (which rightness was only to be recognized in retrospect and would be known by the children's future success and happiness) was added the anxiety of filling the requirements of the role of housewife. In my case, this meant the role of the "doctor's wife" in a small midwestern town. In the post World War II world of family "Togetherness" and "Can

This Marriage Be Saved," certainly there was little doubt about what that role entailed. It was all too clear. The trouble was rather in supposing that every woman would—or should—be able to play this role successfully.

In the growing restlessness and tension that gathered behind the calm facade of middle-class life, a desperate need emerged for finding out what was "wrong" with me and with my marriage. For years I explored, with the understanding acceptance of my psychiatrist, the way that I responded to the circumstances of my life. How strange, I felt, to find that no matter what the circumstances, I seemed to have reacted in predictable ways. So, after lengthy analysis, I continued my life without having discovered the ultimate reason that kept me from being who I was "supposed" to be, but strengthened by the knowledge that I, like my psychiatrist, could find my way of responding to life's experiences both understandable and acceptable.

As my children grew, I needed to develop interests and involvements of my own. And it was a "need." I now believe that a person whose temperament is highly active needs to "do" something. This is a truth that our society has recognized only in the breach as it watched highly active women whose children were grown and out of their care develop a depression which has been given the name Empty Nest Syndrome. Many of today's young women, who pause in their career development only for a short time devoted to childbearing and nurturing of their smaller families, will never wrestle with this particular devil, but for many of their mothers, child care and housework were their careers, and these careers came to a crashing halt or became unfulfilling when the children were grown. So, while my children were still quite young, I moved into graduate studies in sociology. My interest in human behavior became more academically focused.

My interests were turned, "quite naturally" I can now say in retrospect, toward the differing impact the social environment has on individuals, on the behavior that emerges when the individual is confronted in socialization with particular demands and expectations of his society. It is clear that in every society there are some "misfits" whose reaction to the demands their environment places upon them is seen to be dissonant and aberrant. There are others who seem to thrive in the same environment. What makes the crucial difference?

To such personal experiences as the recognition of the individuality of my children, my acceptance of my "self" as I am and apparently have always been, and my continuing curiosity about the interaction of individuals and society, my introduction to the work on temperament added a new dimension. The implications of the Thomas/Chess work on temperament called forth in me a predictable reaction: "Let's do something about it."

* * * *

We began a relationship of co-therapy and collaboration and enjoyed the rich experience of combining our several interests and moving in new directions.

Having read and reread the methodology and validation of the New York Longitudinal Study, we accepted the actuality of the nine dimensions of temperament. Our next step was to attempt extrapolations from childhood behavior to adult socialized behavior. What we wanted to see was if, and how, temperament persisted into adulthood. Over the past few years, we have not only been led toward answering the question, but we have been drawn toward the uses of this knowledge in family life, work-related areas, and last, but not least, its uses in psychotherapy. We have found this conceptualization of the individual to be richly stimulating and rewarding. Though we have maintained our primary direction toward the knowledge and establishment of individuality and autonomy, we have also been quite pleased with the finding that this really requires the confirming interaction and recognition of another. This book and the applications that we have made of our work with temperament in the adult population are as much the result of the "fit" of our own temperaments as the "fit" of our lives together.

JAYNE BURKS
MELVIN RUBINSTEIN

St. Louis, Missouri
May, 1979

Temperament Styles in Adult Interaction

Applications in Psychotherapy

Part I

A New Approach to Psychosocial Development

1

An Overview of Temperament
in Adult Behavior

The purpose of this book is to present a view of self through study of a bio-psychological subsystem defined as temperament. We see temperament as an inborn dimension of reactivity and activity functioning in the manner of a drive system toward involvement with external objects. In the course of growth and development, the temperament dimensions are influenced by family and social systems, but maintain autonomy in interdependent interaction with these systems. It is this continuity of autonomy of the subsystem as it extends into adulthood that is the particular substance of this study.

Since 1956 a group of psychiatrists in New York, headed by Dr. Alexander Thomas and Dr. Stella Chess, have been carrying on the New York Longitudinal Study (NYLS) of temperament dimensions in children (1-3). As we have followed the work of this group, we have found it stimulating to use this study and its findings as a point of departure from which to consider the implications in terms of adult behavior.

The concept of temperament, as the earlier work with children made quite clear, has been conceived of as the attempt to get at the *how* of behavior, or the *way* that behavior is carried out, rather than the *content* or *motivation* of behavior. Temperament represents the inherent, not learned or habitual, mode of creating behav-

3

ior and responding to the behavior of others. Temperament, in this view, is a component of the individual self that does not emerge in interaction with the environment, but which is already present in the acting and reacting organism.

We are introducing in this work a new concept of temperament in which we conceive of temperament as having certain dynamic consequences which have a motivational aspect. Other psychodynamic theories have viewed interactive behavior as being motivated by drive reduction, by life preservation, or by needs to defend the self. Our work, however, posits that an individual will act to achieve "closure" or gratification for the temperament quality itself. Thus, behavior can be seen as motivated from within, from the kind of temperamental dimensions that are an inherent part of the individual and from the struggle to maintain this autonomy of temperament in the process of interaction with the environment.

During the years that the New York Longitudinal Study has been studying temperament, the idea of temperament as a component of behavior has been increasingly accepted. Many behavioral scientists, as well as child psychiatrists, have become interested in the concept a sizable literature has been developed around the concept of temperament in children (4-8).

In spite of the growing interest in this aspect of child behavior, there has not been a concomitant interest in the implications of this study for adult behavior. Temperament, of course, has been the focus of many other studies of adult behavior in terms of personality and of establishing temperament indices of individuals. There are temperament inventories which are useful tools in psychological testing (9-12). It is our purpose in writing this book, however, to report our application of the concepts of temperament, as developed by the NYLS, in the adult population. In using their work as the springboard for our own work, we feel we owe a great debt to the directors of this study for the careful and painstaking investigative study that they have carried out. However, we see our work as proceeding in a different direction. We are not attempting to simply continue the study of temperament in an older age group. Thomas and Chess have themselves now moved into the adult age group as they continue their work. Rather, our work attempts to apply what we see as the implications of their study of temperament for adult behavior. Many of our emerging ideas about the workings of temperament in adults are hypotheses generated from case study material. In terms of empirical research, we look upon our work as a preliminary, inductive approach to the study of temperament in adults. The more systematic testing and verification of the hypotheses that we have developed are, of course, the province of survey research with its much more rigorous methodology.

Temperament, particularly its dynamics in adult behavior, is our primary focus. Having said that, we want to make it clear that we do not see temperament as the only, or even the most important, determinant of behavior. We stress temperament in order to consider the effect of this heretofore rather neglected component in the dynamics of adult behavior; *we are not trying to stress the primacy of temperament over other aspects*. We have, in effect, tried to hold other variables which affect behavior constant while we investigate the way in which the factor of temperament operates in individual behavior. Thus, we may appear to be overstating the case for the influence of temperament, but we are doing so only in the context of focusing our investigation of the dynamics of behavior on this variable. In each individual, the other physical, psychological, and social factors of his life are also assumed to be playing their parts in the construction of that individual's behavior.

The entire scope of our clinical and theoretical work for the past four years has been dedicated to the development of our understanding of temperament in adults. Every patient seen for ongoing individual or group therapy has been viewed, and responded to by us, in the light of temperament and has been made explicitly aware of the substance of our theoretical approach. This has now amounted to hundreds of patients and thousands of patient-hours.

We also have gathered pertinent data outside of the therapeutic setting. We have made numerous workshop presentations to child care and family agency personnel, teachers, social workers, counselors, business and administrative people. In all cases, we have found that individuals understand and respond rather quickly to the substance of our approach. Both in therapeutic and non-therapeutic settings our procedural structure has been constant: 1) didactic explanation;

2) self-identification; 3) group feedback; 4) further self-examination and response; 5) explanation of the interactive importance of communication. We have yet to encounter a situation where we were not able to make the concept of temperament understood and where self-identification was not attempted.

We have presented our work to numerous colleagues, at formal meetings and seminars, as well as in informal discussions. Their responses, often understanding and encouraging, seem at times to indicate to us that we have ventured into an area that, while seemingly peaceful and familiar, is booby-trapped with leftover land mines of past wars—the booby traps of constitutionality, of labeling, of determinism.

NINE DIMENSIONS OF TEMPERAMENT

In continuing the work with temperament done by the NYLS into the adult age group, we have elected to use their nine dimensions describing temperament in children. We have extrapolated the kinds of behavior which manifested temperament in children into more mature manifestations.

Each of the nine dimensions is seen as a continuum on which an individual can be located in terms of his *way* of acting. In Chapter 6 we will enlarge our description of adult behavioral manifestations of temperament dimensions. Briefly, these dimensions and their childhood manifestations as described in the NYLS, as well as the way we see them in adults, are as follows:

1. *Activity Level*: In children, this is the amount of movement the child displays and the proportion of time in a day spent in activity. In adults, we find activity level can include both the amount of activity *and* the kind of mental activity that go with active solutions. The highly active adult is concerned with the question, "What is to be done?"

2. *Rhythmicity*: In the study of children, this dimension is observed in the regularity of bodily functions and of active and inactive periods. The continuum can be seen as one of predictability and unpredictability. In adults, we have discovered that this dimension

can be observed as the preference for routine behavior and the feeling of discomfort when routines or regular expectations are disrupted.

3. *Approach or Withdrawal*: This dimension is observed in positive or negative responses when new stimuli are introduced to the child. We find that this temperament dimension in adults is similar to the childhood responses. Positive reactions to new experiences or new people can be observed as readiness to engage, while negative, or withdrawal, behavior is seen as reluctance, refusal, or cautiousness in new situations.

4. *Adaptability*: In children, this dimension is observed in terms of the ease with which initial reactions can be altered in the face of pressure for a different direction. Adults can be identified as quick-to-adapt if they readily "tune in" to the desires of others and go along with their position. Those who are slow-to-adapt resist conforming to the pressures from others and maintain their own position.

5. *Threshold of Responsiveness*: This was observed in the NYLS study in the intensity of a sensory stimulus needed to evoke a response, whatever that response might be. In adults, we are interested in the alertness to changes in the environment, including change in the social environment. We observe how quickly an individual picks up and responds to the moods or nuances of others or to the surrounding social ambience, as well as how readily he responds to new sensory stimuli.

6. *Intensity*: This continuum, from low to high intensity, indicates the energy level of responsiveness in children. In adults, also, we identify level of intensity in terms of forcefulness and the involvement with which the individual responds to people or situations. As in children, intensity can be displayed throughout the repertoire of responses—the intense adult can be intensely morose as well as intensely euphoric.

7. *Quality of Mood*: In children, this dimension is observed in the proportion of pleasant, smiling, happy behavior as against unpleasant or crying behavior. In adults, we think of positive quality of mood individuals as those who appear to have a "global" enjoyment of their surroundings, as contrasted to those negative quality of mood people who are very "selective" in their expressions of enjoyment.

The words "optimistic" and "pessimistic" in outlook come to mind.

8. *Distractibility*: In children, the NYLS observed the effectiveness of new stimuli in interrupting and altering behavior which was in progress. In adults, we also observe the readiness of the individual to leave an activity and get into another activity.

9. *Persistence*: In children, the length of time an activity is carried out and the resistance to obstacles which would interfere with the activity are considered related. Our persistent adults do not seem to recognize when enough has been said or done. They continue with an activity beyond a level that others consider sufficient. Those with low persistence usually have trouble remaining engaged in an activity unless they are prompted or pressured by those in their social environment.

It has been our observation that not all of the nine dimensions can be identified or evaluated in every individual. It is more common for our respondents to be able to immediately relate to some of the dimensions as particularly meaningful to them, while on other dimensions they are not aware of just how they see themselves. So we find that we can limit ourselves to working with the individual in terms of the dimensions that are particularly salient for him. We consider that other dimensions are relatively minor components or, at least, not important to the individual at that particular juncture of his life when we have come in contact with him.

CLUSTERS OF TEMPERAMENT DIMENSIONS IN CHILDREN

In the earlier work with children, three different constellations or *groupings* of temperament dimensions were identified. These three clusters in the NYLS were referred to as *Easy Children, Difficult Children,* and *Slow-to-Warm-Up Children.* Certain expectations or predictions could be formulated about children who were identified as having one of these temperament clusters.

Easy Children, making up about 40 percent of the NYLS sample, were said to be regular (i.e. high level of rhythmicity), quick to adapt, positive in quality of mood, and mildly or moderately intense. Children with a temperament constellation of irregularity (i.e.

low level of rhythmicity), who withdrew from new situations, were slow to adapt, had a fairly low quality of mood, and showed a high level of intensity were considered Difficult Children. They included about 10 percent of the children in the sample. The Slow-to-Warm-Up Children were also fairly slow in terms of adaptability, but were less intense in expression and more regular in their bodily functions than the Difficult Children. This group comprised 15 percent of the sample.

These groupings accounted for about 65 percent of the NYLS sample of children, leaving us to assume that the other 35 percent of the sample had temperament identities that did not readily match with the three major clusters described.

STYLE CLUSTERS IN ADULTS

In our work with adults, we have found that certain constellations or groupings of the nine dimensions will appear repeatedly in different individuals, allowing us to identify these constellations as styles of behavior. We have identified six different styles of behavior, each composed of a fairly predictable grouping of positions on several different dimensions.

We have not tried to quantify the proportion of our study population who fall into each of our six groups. Although we have observed a preponderance of individuals falling into particular style clusters, we feel this may not be indicative of the proportions found in the general population, since our study group is made up largely of people who have presented themselves for psychiatric treatment and thus cannot be considered a representative group of the adult population.

Without asserting that these six style clusters are an exhaustive list of all possible adult temperament styles, we believe that they have provided us with a conceptual and operational tool for identification of an individual's style. In working with the six clusters, we have been able to observe the component of temperamental style in adult behavior.

For reasons of simplification we have given our six style clusters the names of the most salient temperament dimension in each cluster. In Chapters 8 and 9, a full development of each style, with illustrative case materials, is presented. Briefly, the six style clusters which have emerged in our work with adults are as follows:

1. *The Withdrawer*: This style includes the dimensions of withdrawal (on the Approach-Withdrawal continuum), slow-to-adapt tendency, a fairly low or selective quality of mood, and middle-to-low level of intensity. When the Withdrawer is presented with a new situation, he tends to move away or hold back, often expressing this in oppositionality. Such a person often tries to control situations or people around him, and is cautious or worried about possible untoward contingencies. People with this style cluster are frequently very role conscious since the structure of role behavior gives them the sense of knowing what to do and to expect of others. The Withdrawer is a careful, thoughtful, thorough person who can be relied upon to render a knowledgeable and realistic decision.

2. *The Persister*: Besides a high level of persistence, this style includes a tendency to be slow-to-adapt, a selective quality of mood, and sometimes a high level of distractibility. It is difficult for the Persister to tolerate interruption or input from others. Although he may sense himself as isolated, he takes pride in the fact that he is regarded as a perfectionist, since he is never completely satisfied that he has persisted long enough.

3. *The Intenser*: This style cluster includes, in addition to a high level of intensity, a low threshold of responsiveness, moderate to high persistence, and a quality of mood that varies. Intensers feel and express themselves with great forcefulness. Although they are valued for their aura of excitement, others may experience them as overreacting. They sometimes present themselves for treatment as needing tranquilizers since they feel themselves to be unstable.

4. *The Approacher*: When new stimuli are presented, the Approacher seldom hesitates to become involved. However, unless stimulated, he will have a low level of activity. The cluster also includes a low threshold of response. The Approacher is quick-to-adapt and has a fairly low, or selective, quality of mood. His ready responsiveness and adaptability can make him steadfast and loyal, but sometimes leave him a hapless victim of exploitation.

5. *The Adapter*: The most important dimension is a quick adap-

tiveness, usually accompanied by a fairly high level of distractibility. With a higher level of activity than the Approacher and a more positive, global, quality of mood, Adapters are generally pleasing companions and good group people. Because they generally go along with others, they rarely assert their own position and tend to resist, if they resist at all, in a passive, covert way.

6. *The Doer*: This style cluster includes a high level of activity with middle to high intensity. Achievement, problem solving, and success all loom large for the Doer. His quality of mood seems variable, generally expressed as apprehension and anxiety before completing an activity, and satisfaction when the task is finished. Because of the overriding importance of activity, the Doer may seem somewhat slow to adapt, particularly if this could mean giving up his plan of action.

In the descriptions of the style clusters that we have developed in working with adults, we have suggested the dynamic consequences of temperament. In observing the manifestations of temperament dimensions, we have perceived that the individual appears to *strive* to display his temperament identity. He is not a *tabula rasa* upon which social behavior is imposed by the environment; rather, his behavior includes the component of *how* the individual is being that self. As he responds to his environment, as he learns to play his reciprocal role in interaction, he perpetuates the *style* of his temperament.

TEMPERAMENT IN INTERACTION

In the NYLS, parental recognition and acceptance of a child's temperament dimensions were considered important in whether parent-child dissonance and consequent emotional distress would occur. In adults, we have postulated that the consonance or dissonance of relationships will be seen in the context of the *mutual* recognition and acceptance of temperament. We have found that the lack of fit of temperaments in interaction may be due, in part, simply to the fact that certain styles do not mesh well with certain other styles. But also, and perhaps more importantly, the ability to recognize and accept temperament appears to be the basis of consonant relationships in adult interaction. Thus, we consider the process of *communicating* temperament styles in social interaction to be as important as the process of *identifying* temperament in an individual.

In our clinical applications of the concepts of temperament, we consider as preliminary information the investigation as to the position of an individual on the nine continua of temperament dimensions and the identification of the style cluster that the individual typically displays. With this information, we then proceed to work with our clients in terms of the way their particular style of behavior can be communicated to others for their recognition and acceptance. We have postulated that if an individual's sytle is not recognized and allowed in interaction, then that particular interactive encounter will not bring about a sense of gratification which we think of as "closure." Since all persons in an interactive event are presenting their individual styles (as well as their cognitive stance, social role understanding, and other components of behavior) , then satisfactory social relationships which are ongoing will depend upon the mutual confirmation and support of the styles which are involved.

Further, our experience indicates that temperament styles, because they are seen as inherent and natural tendencies to behave in certain ways, are sometimes used in inappropriate or nonproductive ways. At such times, the recognition and communication from another can be reparative to the individual and can be seen as helpful in restoring or reestablishing a more appropriate use of the individual's style. In later chapters, we will deal especially with these aspects of the use of the communication of temperament in interaction.

Identification of individual temperament dimensions and styles, communication for the purpose of confirmation and support, and the knowledge of the interactive consequences of temperament (in self and others) form the basic framework of this study and the three-part way in which we apply the implications of temperament as we work with adults. It is out of this framework that we have formulated some new and nontraditional theoretical positions on the psychodynamics of behavior, as well as some new and nontraditional views of individual behavior in interaction with the larger society, which are described in Chapters 2 and 3.

REFERENCES

1. THOMAS, A., CHESS, S., BIRCH, H. G., HERTZIG, M., and KORN, S. *Behavioral Individuality in Early Childhood.* New York: New York University Press, 1963.
2. THOMAS, A., CHESS, S., and BIRCH, H. G. *Temperament and Behavior Disorders in Children.* New York: New York University Press, 1968.
3. THOMAS, A. and CHESS, S. *Temperament and Development.* New York: Brunner/Mazel, 1977.
4. CADORET, R. J., CUNNINGHAM, L., LUFTUS, R., and EDWARDS, J. Studies of adoptees from psychiatrically disturbed biologic parents. *Journal of Pediatrics,* 1975, 87: 301-306.
5. CAREY, W. B. Clinical applications of infant temperament measurement. *Journal of Pediatrics,* 1972, 81:823-828.
6. GARSIDE, R. J., BIRCH, H., SCOTT, D. McI., CHAMBERS, S., KOLVIN, I., TWEDDLER, E. G., and BARBER, L. M. Dimensions of temperament in infant school children. *Journal of Child Psychology and Psychiatry,* 1975, 16:219-231.
7. GRAHAM, P., RUTTER, M., and GEORGE, S. Temperamental characteristics of predictors of behavior disorders in children. *American Journal of Orthopsychiatry,* 43:328-339.
8. SAMEROFF, A. J. Early influences on development: Fact or fancy? *Merrill-Palmer Quarterly of Behavior and Development,* 1975, Vol. 21, No. 4.
9. BUSS, A. H. and PLOMIN, R. *A Temperament Theory of Personality Development.* New York: John Wiley & Sons, 1975.
10. GUILFORD, J. P. and ZIMMERMAN, W. S. *The Guilford-Zimmerman Temperament Survey: Manual of Directions and Norms.* Beverly Hills, CA: Sheridan Supply, 1955.
11. THORNDIKE, R. L. *Thorndike Dimensions of Temperament: Manual.* New York: The Psychological Corporation, 1966.
12. *Thurstone Temperament Schedule: Examiner's Manual.* Chicago: Science Research Associates, 1950.

2

The Psychodynamics
of Temperament

The development of a new view of the psychodynamics of behavior was certainly not a goal we had foreseen in our work with the concepts of temperament. This view has emerged from the continuing observations of temperament in adults in our clinical work.

THE SEARCH FOR A PREVENTIVE APPROACH

When we first read of the work of Thomas, Chess, et al., we found our interest heightened by the idea that their methodology could show the existence of given temperament dimensions from behavioral responses in the individual child. Satisfied on this score, we then turned to their clinical evidence of the significance of temperament for behavior disorders. Here the authors unveiled, to our knowledge for the first time in child psychology literature, the exciting concept that the behavior disorders they encountered in their sample group were largely associated with parent-child dissonance around the child's temperament. We were immediately stimulated by the prospect of a simple, yet effective, system of preventive psychiatry.

Given the possibility of early infantile temperament identification, it might be possible for parents to use this knowledge about the child in respect to their child's growth and development. With the recognition of the child's temperament, parents could become engaged

14

in the socialization process in a more consonant and confident way and avoid the emotional distress, for both parents and children, of dissonance. We decided to see if we could plan some way to begin moving toward this preventive direction.

Our first thoughts centered on the parental component of dissonance, since we viewed parent-child dissonance as the prime target of a preventive approach. When we considered what seemed to be reasons for parental non-acceptance of their child's temperament, we began to examine the possibility of a conflict of temperaments, a poor fit. Since we accepted the work of the NYLS as substantiating the early presence of temperament dimensions, it then seemed logical to see if there was continuity of temperament dimensions in adults from childhood on. If that were so, it should be possible to identify these adult dimensions and then encourage parental self-awareness in order to avoid dissonance. We decided, therefore, to use our new awareness of temperament in psychotherapy sessions with our patients. Since we were particularly interested in the issue of persistence of temperament, we chose to remain with the nine dimensions of temperament formulated by the NYLS and to see if our patients were able to identify themselves on these dimensions. As we gathered these observations, we also became aware that adult responses tended to group themselves generally into the six style clusters mentioned earlier.

Temperament Styles in Some Psychotherapy Patients

Following along with the assumptions of the NYLS that temperament dimensions are aspects of behavior that an individual brings to the interactive situation, we were prepared to accept temperament as an inherent style, having little to do with the development of pathological behavior patterns. Pathological behavior is generally considered to be caused through neurochemical processes having a relatively fixed effect, or as a symptom coming out of conflict, or as a result of faulty ego development. An inherent temperament style would not seem to be a part of any of these views of pathology. Yet we were able to observe that temperament styles seemed to be involved in the way our patients described their behavior. The following examples will demonstrate the way that temperament styles appeared in some of our patients.

Patients whom we had identified as having *Withdrawer* temperament styles habitually engaged in controlling kinds of behavior in their interpersonal relations. As therapists, we came to expect from them an initially hostile, querulous and highly confronting approach. There were attempts to maneuver us into defensive reactions. Spouses and children of these people were treated in much the same way. They were admonished by the Withdrawer to act only with his prior approval, which was rarely given.

A number of patients identified as having a *Doer* style cluster surprised us by avoiding doing. They habitually avoided entering into and completing action toward accomplishment, showing a heightened anxiety about possibilities of failure and a readiness to give up in the face of any challenge.

Adapters who seemed bent on agreeing with and pleasing almost everyone secretly entertained thoughts widely divergent from those ascribed to them and would often behave in ways unfathomable to those who thought they knew them. Families were often confused by behavior contrary to their social expectations. All the while, these Adapters maintained their agreeableness.

Intensers were often encountered who seethed quietly while giving the bug-eyed impression of capping a volcano. They habitually appeared over-controlled, but would describe occasions when they would burst into intense sexual or violent acting out. Intensers often suffered from accompanying somatic symptoms such as headaches, gastric distress, diarrhea, high blood pressure.

Approachers were seen who habitually hooked themselves into relationships where they were taken advantage of. Filled with feelings of inferiority, they shied away from people known to be successful and stable. Parents felt desperate that the models they tried to imbue their child with were rejected over and over again.

There were *Persisters* who habitually had to have the last word, even if there had been a thousand words too many. They were unsurpassed in their ability to ward off any intrusion from others around them. This was accomplished by an incessant volubility or by a skillful, unbeatable fencing. They would "rather die" than submit to the regulatory intervention of anyone, no matter how benign. They had a single-minded devotion to detail, ritual and process.

In sum, it appeared to us that many of our patients were caught in a process of repressing, skewing or overusing their given temperament style in a striving to attain some sort of recognition. It was as if, in response to non-recognition or dissonance (perhaps stemming from early parental non-recognition or perhaps from present dissonant relations), they were engaged in behavior that would *force* the desired *closure*.

PSYCHOTHERAPEUTIC CONSIDERATIONS

Earlier Psychotherapy: Non-Recognition of Temperament

In retrospect, we began to reflect upon our experience of psychotherapy over many years. There were several groupings of patients whose behavior now seemed more understandable. As is usual in a general psychiatric practice, a large percentage of the patients were women, many of whom came in with similar complaints. They were generally unhappy with themselves, with their marriages, with their assumed roles as wives and mothers. Remembering happier days when they were recognized as lively, energetic and intense young girls, they had discovered that these same traits needed to be curbed after marriage. Intense expressions of feeling were often seen as "hysterical," resulting in their seeking psychiatric treatment. Therapy then began with the pursuit of *why* they were resisting the "normal" role of women and what was the historical reason behind this troublesome behavior. Despite strong efforts to trace back the causative sequence of "pathology," there seemed to be a repetitive element to the distress-producing behavior that defeated the patients' best intentions to change. The usual diagnostic labels of these women, such as narcissistic or hysterical character neuroses, were lacking an essential intrinsic component of self. An element of individuality was being overlooked by a therapeutic system tied to the imposition of traditional sexual roles.

Another grouping of patients who had appeared in significant numbers were young adult males presenting complaints of feeling adrift, without goals, and gripped by anomie. Having adapted to a masculine ideal (often actually epitomized by their fathers), they discovered they could not satisfactorily sustain these goals. Lack of motivation in children of strongly motivated parents was, of course, pathologically suspect and a historical search of Oedipal causation of such resistance was begun. It was apparent, however, as with the unhappy wives, that the difficulties arose from individual styles that had been in existence for as long as the patients could remember, but were now considered inappropriate and unacceptable. Though they tried hard to change, they seemed not to know *how* to change.

Work with parents further pointed up some therapeutic problems. Having accepted the dictum that they themselves were responsible for frustrating proper instinctual development, parents began rearing their children in accordance with the best dynamic principles. When the child's behavior outcome was troublesome, parents blamed themselves and sought professional advice to straighten out their failure. Despite extensive efforts to restructure parent-child relationships, behavioral traits of their children that were unacceptable to these parents tended to hang on. Again, it seemed that we were dealing with an intrinsic factor in the child, an individuality that resisted any manipulation towards change.

It appeared that theories of personality development, including psychoanalytic theory, were overlooking an element of intrinsic individuality.

Psychiatric theory has had a strong reaction against "constitutionality" and has rejected the Kraepelinian pessimism of fixed prognosis that seemed to result from considering the possibilities of inborn dimensions of behavior. There was a preference for psychodynamic theories which seemed to start from an equalized instinctual plane of orality and proceed through genitality. The way these instincts were handled between infants and parents then explained our behavior.

The NYLS was able to show that interference with, or nonacceptance of, temperament dimensions produced a state of dissonance which often led to behavior disorders in children. It seemed that our observations of problem behavior in adults, which included the component of strong striving for temperament style recognition, could indicate a concomitant state of dissonance due to interference or nonacceptance.

As we thought more in terms of the role of temperament, we began to see the possibility that we were dealing with a dynamic drive system, biologically based, of a nonsexual nature. It appeared that much of the behavior seen in our patients could be understood on the basis of the centrality of their style clusters and their need to sustain decisive elements of their individuality. A great deal of what we experienced as habitual psychopathological reactions now became quite comparable to manifestations of "character" in the psychoanalytic framework.

Psychodynamics of Ego Psychology

Character, as defined psychoanalytically, is the habitual reactivity that becomes recognized as "typical, or "characteristic," of that person. Our reactions become arranged into subliminal or unconscious habituations. From the point of view of survival, this may be most desirable. If reactions are organized to function quickly and without too much thinking, a system is established which is close to the instinctual system of animal behavior. Ego psychology has made us aware of the human developmental tendency toward diminution of consciousness of perception and response; a basic principle of ego functioning is that behavior is directed toward bringing comfort. In the psychoanalytic view, character has been seen as emanating from the defensive functions of the ego. Infantile conflict, with its attendant affect states such as anxiety, guilt and sadness, was handled by the establishment of a defensive reactivity, which became characteristic and which set up a level of existential comfort and subconscious self-perception. What we were seeing, then, were *styles* of behavior. But, in Freudian terms, they were thought to be largely the outcome of the defensive system and they bore that system's identification marks. Defenses such as reaction formation, denial, or displacement, to name a few, were thought to be discerned in the characterological behavior. Behind all of this ego representation was the instinctual life, largely conceptualized as sexual libido. Ego psychology rested basically on the biologically based libido and the subsequent affect-laden conflicts around libidinous objects and goals.

Psychodynamics of Temperament

Our position, like the psychoanalytic view, is strongly biologically based. However, instead of assuming only the dominant universal presence of libidinous energy in a drive system, we assume the presence of a nonsexual system oriented toward *how* an individual functions and copes with his environment. This system, composed of a number of dimensions of acting and reacting (the nine temperament dimensions), is inherent and can be seen as an individual's *style*. In the sense that we can observe the individual consistently manifesting his style in his interactions with his environment, we could think of this style as being characteristic. The temperament system is not amorphous but is highly differentiated. The dimensions can be thought of as autonomous, yet interlinked into style clusters that form the infant's basic self-identity. We believe that one element of organization of behavior is to preserve and maintain the actuality of the temperament style. The temperament system seeks closure, which is seen as a gratifying response of recognition and acceptance from others. The drive towards closure leads to the display of the temperament style which is dominant in such a way that others can respond.

In infancy, the system is highly sensitive to parental response. An ungratifying, disagreeable response in parent-child interaction is conceptualized as dissonant. Rather than postulate conflict around a symbolic, mythologized extrapolation of sexuality, we see the dissonance as the result of an ill-fitting interaction of the parental self and the developing infant self. In adults, the style of behavior of an individual continues to seek closure, now from the nonparental social responses. Again, dissonant relationships will occur when such responses are not forthcoming.

Thus, our psychotherapy patients could be understood in this framework to be acting towards the achievement of their own autonomy and the sense of gratification, or closure, in interaction with others.

In the same way that defensive characterological motivations have become subconscious, much of the temperament *style* of an individual has become manifested in ways that are automatic and habitual, and thus not conscious. It is our belief that bringing temperament dimensions of an individual to the conscious level and helping the person to recognize the ways in which he displays his temperament in interactions with others are vital steps in a therapeutic approach.

While we have proceeded in our development of the psychodynamics of temperament from therapeutic applications, we feel that this study is by no means limited to the consideration of pathology. In viewing our patients from the standpoint of their temperaments, we have dropped any orientation to their behavior as "sick." We have a conception of "normal" behavior that includes the very real possibility that interaction at all stages of life can result in consonant or dissonant effects. We see behavior as interactive—not only in early developmental stages, but throughout adult life as well. And temperament is a very important component in that interactive process.

SOME CLINICAL CASES

The following clinical examples illustrate the difference in the traditional psychodynamic interpretation of case history material and the temperament style dynamics that we have been using. In these cases, the traditional view would be concerned with showing the symptomatic behavior of the individual as proceeding from the earlier stages of psychosocial development and would infer a cause-and-effect dynamics. By getting back to the original traumatic childhood stages, one can attempt to explain later difficulties in interpersonal behavior. In the temperament style view, the present behavior is seen as the stylistic expression of the individual. The earlier history is looked on as corroborative of the presence of this style as a factor in the development of dissonance. The dissonance is seen as directly related to nonrecognition and need not continue if the individual can establish relationships which are accepting and supportive.

Jean

Jean, a 30-year-old woman, came for therapy because of concern about her marriage. She was submitting to pressure from a husband who was unhappy with her pattern of social and personal withdrawal. Though her coming seemed at his insistence, she did wonder, albeit defensively, whether something might not be wrong with her. She had a lifelong history of difficulties in entering into interpersonal relationships, experiencing what to her was initial overwhelming, paralyzing anxiety. She hated her father, whom she saw as an insensitive brute who had brow-beaten her from childhood.

The traditional psychodynamic formulation might be as follows. Jean's character structure was substantially developed through the projective mode of defense. She constantly feared, and seemed to accept, the strong prescience that others found her or her work unsatisfactory and were always on the verge of criticizing her. Though she generally withdrew, there was an acerbic, querulous reactive element, with which she challenged even the friendliest of approaches as having hidden rejective intentions. Her verbalizations pointed to strong oral sadistic tendencies. These might represent a fixation on that psycho-sexual level brought about by parental reaction against the intense aggressive instinctual activity of the oral stage. She is extremely frightened of the build-up of intense feelings, sexual as well as aggressive, and defends basically by withdrawal rein-forced by projection.

Viewing Jean from the perspective of her temperament style, we would see her as a Withdrawer who from birth experienced all new interpersonal situations as fraught with anxiety; her reaction initially and instantly was to complain and withdraw. Her mother, a strongly inhibited Doer, went along with the withdrawal while her father, a strongly role-determined With-drawer, attempted to stimulate her by rather harsh, shaming statements. This aroused more intense withdrawal on her part. After a period of combat, father would slink away defeated. Almost all interpersonal relationships were seen in the context of this combat, and therapy was experienced by us initially as a battle. Her relationship with her husband was also dominated by a strong, initial "NO!" typical of the oppositionality of the Withdrawer.

Tracy

Tracy is a 21-year-old woman who, after an intense period of adolescent sexual acting-out, has established a satisfying adult relationship with her parents and is working steadily at a job where she is highly valued and liked. She is second of four children, the only one considered a problem child. School was a painful, arduous experience marked by few successes and great resistance. As a child, she was intensely argumentative about her mother's directions ("Why do I have to do that?") and reiterated feeling of alienation by screaming, "I am not like the rest of them" (her brothers and sisters). Father's interactions introduced more ambivalence as he was both strongly authoritative and at times indulgent. In her later years of high school, she joined with a group considered outcasts and misfits, shifting into an impulse-ridden life where she eventually became pregnant, carried the infant to term, and relinquished it. After delivery, Tracy returned home, shortly thereafter developing the stable responses mentioned earlier.

From the traditional psychoanalytic point of view, Tracy might be seen as having difficulty in handling the ambivalence around anal levels of infantile sexuality. She could be intensely positive as well as negative, but negative expressions were experienced as potentially destructive. Her parents reacted strongly in their wish to see everyone as calmly well adjusted. Repression seemed faulty, leading to repeated breakthroughs that culminated in extensive impulsive behavior. During her adolescence, her preoccupation with her identity crisis left her with little defensive strength. A close, accepting support from her mother made it possible for her to heal through identification with the love object she could now begin to incorporate.

From the point of view of temperament style, we would say that Tracy was born an Intenser. Her mother was a middle-active Doer who saw herself as creating a happy childhood for her children. She responded to Tracy's intense outbursts as if this were some dissonant state she had caused or "should be able to do something about." Instead of gaining recognition for her intense feelings and mode of expression, Tracy experienced nonacceptance and alienation. She experienced the negative side of her intensity as evidence that she was incapable and rarely sought or received support to continue her struggles to closure and a satisfactory outcome. Her acting-out can be seen as a skewed attempt to gain recognition for herself from other alienated people. What was particularly healing here was Tracy's asking her parents for reassuring help during the last fearful months of her pregnancy and her mother's positive, accepting response. The episode over and the painful intensity mastered, Tracy now was able to consider further excursions into effective living with the added protection of asking for and accepting help when needed.

Robert

Robert is a 40-year-old man who came to therapy because his second marriage seemed to be steadily dissolving into continuous episodes of emotionally intense recriminations. After a period of inner containment of tension and worry, he would finally erupt into a series of accusations about his wife's extravagances and mismanagement and his children's dissolute, self-serving behavior. He was an only child who had been made largely responsible for a family business at the age of 17 when his father died. He worked hard trying to carry out his charge of taking care of his mother and, a few short years later, his first wife and growing family. His mother at last turned the business over to him directly. Some years later, aware of incessant unhappiness, he divorced his wife and married a woman with whom he thought he could be very happy. He has adopted her children from a previous marriage and, in his attempt to bring the good life to everyone, is working harder than ever. It is extremely difficult for him to relinquish control over his business activities and to delegate the necessary authority for others to responsibly get their job done.

A traditional psychodynamic explanation might see Robert, an only child, as being involved in intense rivalry with his father for the maternal Oedipal sex object. The resolution of the Oedipal conflict resulted in Robert's denial of rivalry and his assumption of a more passive, dependent relationship to his parents. With the death of his father occurring at the height of adolescent resurgence, Robert unconsciously felt as if he had victoriously disposed of his rival. The role he now assumed, as man of the house, conflicted substantially with the older passive, dependent character structure. He experienced a good deal of anxiety about his assumption of this new role, fearing his plans would be sabotaged by others. This led to work behavior which steadily denied his dependent needs. Eventually he would blow up, making recriminative demands on others.

Using the temperament dynamics of style, we would say that Robert was born a Doer. There seemed to be little dissonance around his childhood "doing" behavior up until the abrupt demise of his father. At that time, it became necessary for him to assume premature responsibility, and he evidenced a great deal of anxiety around possible failure. He expanded his activity in the quest for recognition, but apparently did little to communicate his anxiety. The inadequacy of the maternal response seemed to imply he was not doing enough, leading to redoubling of his efforts. His activity has always been directed toward manipulating gratifying responses from others, but in doing so, he never carries out his style toward what he wants to do for his own sense of closure and fulfillment.

The examples have been presented here to make clear the difference in temperament theory and psychoanalytic theory. The advantage, as we see it, of using temperament theory lies in accepting the individual as he now sees himself and as he has been in the past. We see the person as strongly interactively involved from the start and not necessarily as just a victim of external impositions on his instinctual life. It is our intention to present an alternative to the psychoanalytic view.

3

The Social Psychology of Temperament

As the continuing study of temperament began to make us aware of the new view we were developing about the psychodynamics of behavior, we also began to realize that the component of temperament had been largely ignored in the development of theories in social psychology. Social psychology, while its focus is mainly on the effect of the social environment on the behavior of the individual, must also take into account the effect of individuals on the society in which they live. The society is not only in the individual in determining the behavior that the individual will construct; individuals and their needs are in the society, determine the shape of the society and bring about changes in the society.

Although social psychologists do not leave out the impact of the individual organism in their formulations of the development of a social self, the individual is seen as coming into the world largely undifferentiated. The "self" emerges out of the process of social interaction and the first glimmerings of self-identity come with the realization that needs are answered by some external non-self. In the continuing interaction of the self and the social group, the self-identity becomes established and the symbolic meanings of behavior become validated in the group experience. The contribution of the infant organism itself, in terms of active or reactive behavior, comes

26

to be disregarded in such a view. Behavior which is thought of as *characteristic* of the individual is seen as coming out of the process of socialization. A child who typically (characteristically) retreats from new stimuli can be seen as "being afraid" and the reasons for his fear may be sought in some earlier frightening experience which *caused* him to be afraid. The idea that it is natural and inherent for him to withdraw from new stimulation has no place in such a theoretical position.*

But this is not the only theoretical position that neglects to think of the individual as other than a social construct. Role theory shows individual behavior to be the result of certain expectations imposed by functional requirements. In any given society, certain functions must be performed and individuals must be molded to fulfill these expectations. Society and all of its sub-systems are made up of people fulfilling roles, which are required to ensure the preservation of the whole.

Role behavior includes not only the content expected but also the appropriate affect or *way* of playing out the prescribed role. Some latitude around what would be defined as a norm of behavior for a certain role can be accepted so that individual differences can be allowed, if not theoretically accounted for. In such a view, individual variations in the way roles are played which are not within an acceptable range around the norm are seen as deviant and the society must find ways to sanction, punish, or rehabilitate the deviant individual back into the appropriate role behavior. The same behavior may be considered eminently fitting in some roles but shockingly out of line in another role. To think of the possibility that a particular way of acting could be seen as acceptable because it is a "given" aspect of the individual's behavior is to challenge the basic premise of role theory. It is our view that we do not become the set of roles we play. We remain, in temperament dimensions, the self that we were meant to be. Sometimes we are forced by role requirements to repress or

---

* In the last decade and a half there has been evidence of a shift of thinking away from this position, appearing especially in the child development literature. Jerome Bruner, one of the editors of *The Developing Child* series, is among those who emphasize that the newborn does not perceive a "blooming buzzing confusion" but is capable of constructing behavior at any age, even *in utero,* in individual discriminatory ways.

alter our own autonomy or sometimes we risk the designation as deviant as we attempt to actualize ourselves in terms of temperament.

In any society, certain ways of behaving come to be valued more than others. The urbanized, secularized, and industrialized society of America in the 20th century has produced changes in the picture of the social psychology of today's men and women as they live in this particular social environment. As has been suggested numerous times, technological changes spearhead social changes and the pace of technological change since the beginning of the industrial revolution has appeared to increase with each subsequent decade. In the past, social arrangements fitting a technological stage of development have stabilized expected behavior and become institutionalized, providing an environment in which individuals could know what was expected of them and could experience this as security. Institutions, of course, become a stabilizing force in any society as they harden behavior into dogma, into law, and into ritualized manners and customs.

In the view of Talcott Parsons, for example, the structural requirements of the industrial society for mobility of the worker, both geographically and vertically in the socioeconomic class structure, made the small nuclear family a "fitting," therefore "right," norm for the family. In such a society, the large extended family of several generations living in close contact, which suited the technological stage of the earlier agricultural society, is no longer functionally apropos. Thus, the institutional requirements of the nuclear family now supported a view of the behavior to be considered normative: a husband would be the one "worker" (or the primary worker) in the economic sphere, and the exigencies of his occupation would determine the socioeconomic status of the family and the place of residence of the nuclear unit. The wife would be only peripherally engaged in the occupational world, and the occupation of mother and housewife would take primacy. Again, in such a view the particular individualism of the member in such institutions cannot be accommodated.

But when rapid changes occur, the institutionalized norms for behavior lag behind the new social arrangements that are now required. It is now too familiar a fact to again belabor that the institutional arrangements and requirements are out of harmony with the trends of continued urbanization, secularization, and industrialization. Institutions which formerly surrounded us with a stable structure did so because they acquired through consensual validation a moral power. Behavior then became "right" or "wrong" because it served or did not serve institutional requirements. Now, as institutions themselves are responding to the rapid pace of change, they no longer provide the bulwark of correct or moral societal behavior. Individuals are left without the strength of feeling that they know, or have been socialized to believe, what is to be done.

There is a wealth of support for the Durkheimian position that social cohesiveness is related to individual emotional stability. His conclusions, that rates of suicide (as an index to individual emotional stability) correlated with the strength of the religious group in providing a pervasive climate of cohesiveness around individual behavior, have become accepted and repeatedly supported. The plight of the individual deprived of such societal support is that of normlessness or anomie, deprived of his identity as a member of society and having no sense of security in his relationships with others. As we have watched our social institutions undergo the inevitable changes in the face of the overwhelming consequences of technological changes, we have witnessed also the increase of the personal disasters of anomie. We hear it in the injured complaint of the older Army officer who looks askance at the "new individualism" offered as a recruitment bait for an Army which can no longer depend upon conscription. We see it in the revolt of some conservative members of churches who see new modernizations of church practices as a loss of "God's will." We observe it in the efforts of legislators and others to retard or obstruct certain social groups in their efforts to move out of their older institutionalized positions and to insist upon their rights for equal opportunities. To these examples each of us could add numerous others which point up the struggle to accommodate to the normlessness of a society which in many ways has seemed to have lost its center.

In response to the present plight of the individual in society, there seemed to be two opposing points of view: 1) restore the strength of our institutions; 2) equip the individual to find the strength within himself to live in a changing society. As an example of the first position, that of restoring strength of an institution, we would like to discuss the institution of the Family as a case in point. It is rare to pick up a periodical of whatever stripe, "slicks" to "pulps," that does not present an article which attacks the problem of "what is to be done about The Family?" The institution of the Family has probably engendered more copy than any other social issue in the past decade. It is hardly possible to catalogue the diagnoses of *why* the Family has become weakened but the evidence that it *has* become weakened is rehearsed endlessly in the figures of rising divorce rates, falling birth rates, emotional problems of children from broken homes, and a host of other evidences of institutional weakness. The answers, almost as varied as the problems, are mainly toward efforts to strengthen the Family, presumably the traditional family of two parents and their minor children, seen still as the functional requirement of the industrialized society, as stated earlier by Talcott Parsons. Such efforts to come to the assistance of this beleaguered institution are seen in both the public and the private sector. In 1977, The Carnegie Council on Children headed by Kenneth Keniston published their recommendations for strong societal supports of families with children, including such far-reaching proposals as guaranteed income and cutting unemployment among heads of households of such families, including single parent female heads. Now, two years later, there is little sign that these recommendations have been taken seriously in the political and economic institutions although it is difficult to refute the reasoning of this report.

In the private sector, one of the ways of working with troubled families is to view a family as a "system" and, again, to find ways to strengthen the system by analyzing and correcting the roles that individual members play in the family. We find ourselves in wholehearted support of both of these views of the way to deal with families in trouble and have worked ourselves towards the liberal goals suggested by the Keniston study, and the efforts to help family groups improve the overall functioning of their family in "family system" therapy. However, from the standpoint of our study of temperament, we feel that the component of individual temperament styles has played an unrecognized part in the institution of the family. Now, because of the changes that have occurred as society has moved far from the simple "mechanical" structure of agricultural culture to the complex "organic" structure of urbanized society, individualism means more than differentiation on the basis of the division of labor. It is time to think of social systems as not simply sets of roles in interaction but sets of individuals, each of whom will interact in a style which we see as inherent and consistent throughout the life cycle. In a society in which a lowered birth rate and an urbanized life style have made the adult role for women of mother and homemaker a role with decreasing content, then role behavior based on such a view of what adult women do is no longer applicable. If adult males can thus be released from their role of sole economic support of the family, they are freed for sharing other functions in the family and other interests outside the family. If other institutions, educational and political, have taken over, in a professionalization that families cannot match, the functions of socialization of children and the care of aging or infirm family members, then individuals may be held together only because of mutual compatibility. Now, not the *permanence* of a relationship, but the *quality* of a relationship is the mark of successful marriages and families.

In this view of the reality of family functioning, when social changes have emptied family roles of meaningful content, and when social changes are permitting new rights and opportunities for more varied participation of both males and females in economic and personal relationships, the way, or *style,* in which an individual relates to others becomes a new basis for relationships. As shown in the earlier work with children, the interactive recognition of temperament style can strongly influence whether or not parent-child consonance or dissonance will emerge. In our study, we have found a similar result in adult interactions. Adults will find a relationship consonant or dissonant in terms of the mutual recognition and gratification of styles. Therefore, where other societal requirements and constraints on family performance are weakened, the exigencies of individual satisfaction and self actualization based on maintenance of temperament autonomy will increase in importance. The measures which will strengthen family ties and will promote enduring family relationships will need to consider ways in which individuals in a marriage or a family system can recognize and support individual temperament styles. The same conclusion can be asserted when other areas of society are considered. For example, many of the dissatisfactions and problems seen in the occupational world—problems of job turnover, alcoholism, shoddy workmanship, inefficiency and general malfeasance on the job—can be shown to be related to the unwillingness to deal with, or perhaps the failure to consider, the individuality of workers.

There is, however, as mentioned above, another way of viewing the plight of the individual adrift in a rapidly changing society and that is to socialize, or re-socialize, the individual to "adjust" to such a socety. Towards this end, an entire industry has now emerged which goes under the euphemism of the human potential movement. It is labeled in less flattering terms, by those who view it with a jaundiced eye, as The New Narcissism. It seems to be the goal of this movement to show individuals how to be *effective* in their interactions with others and leads to a host of books, courses, and advicegiving on the subject of how to obtain desired goals for oneself. The goals are, of course, the societal ones of being successful, winning, being an effective parent or leader, and in general making sure that one puts one's own interests first and forthrightly pursues them. The means for obtaining these goals are myriad: improve communication skills; assert oneself; rid oneself of crippling "hang-ups" (this may include recreating one's own birth with an accompanying primal scream, or unlocking a postural or muscular tightness by massage which sometimes becomes vigorous enough to resemble a beating.)

While it is easy enough to criticize this current trend and to use the label of narcissism to belittle the search for gratification that underlies the various manifestations of this movement, it is harder to recognize that it expresses a search for some way to cope with a society in which rapid change has taken away the old social cohesiveness that provided, if not a constraint, at least a measuring stick by which behavior could be judged. If old norms of socially accepted behavior no longer apply and old institutions have lost their power to be morally compelling, then how can social interaction be entered into except in terms of self-interest?

It is at this point that a new view of individuality, including an inherent component of temperament, can enter the arena of the individual's interaction with his social environment. The view that a person presents himself interactively with an individual style and that he must receive interactive recognition and confirmation of that style in order to sense himself as a fully autonomous person is our view of the place of temperament style in social psychology. The individual is not the product of the social environment, nor the hapless servant of its institutional requirements. But neither is he the independent actor who manipulates his social environment for his own narcissistic ends. Rather, he is a social being, responsive to the society in which he lives but bringing to the interaction a way of acting which strives for the confirmation of his individuality.

4

Methodology: Issues and Praxis

In any study, the methods that are used will in some way guide and direct the conclusions that are drawn. Conclusions must always be considered in light of the way in which they have been obtained. So it is important to describe the methodology of a study and the circumstances under which the study was carried out. In the best scientific sense, the chances for bias and unwarranted results can be minimized by electing methods which hold strictly to the requirements for objectivity, reliability, and validation. But testing for verification is only one side of the research endeavor; the development of new ideas and theories often requires different methods.

We are reporting case studies of some of our work and thus many of our emerging ideas about the workings of temperament in adults can be seen as hypotheses generated from case study material. We are aware that our own methods of study have been more qualitative than quantitative and our observations have encouraged subjective as well as objective reporting. For this reason, we find ourselves taking positions and making assumptions that objective and quantitative measures might find very difficult to deal with. Among the most difficult of these issues is that of the persistence and continuity of temperament dimensions in an individual through various stages of growth and development. Because temperament does interact with

34

various other factors, both internal and external, as the individual grows, the observable behavior reflects this interaction in a variety of ways. The more clear-cut manifestations of temperament, apparent very early in life, certainly do not remain constant.

The problem is similar to that involved in the study of attitudes and may be, as in that area, a problem of validation. For example, if in response to a questionnaire a known "attitude score" on a specific attitude under study can be ascertained, then that score should be predictive of some behavioral consequences. Yet when behavior related to the attitude in question is observed, it is very difficult to obtain significant expected correlations with known attitude scores of the subjects. Unless we are willing to forego entirely the study of attitudes, because of this difficulty of validation, we must assume that there are "intervening variables" between the individual's attitudinal set and his behavior.

In a similar way, we can postulate that direct observations of behavior at a very early age can be undertaken and temperament dimensions quantified on the basis of these observations. Direct observations of appropriately *similar* behavior (not, of course, the same behavior) at a later stage of development might yield little significant correlation to the earlier observed temperament "score" and thus make it very difficult to demonstrate persistence of temperament. We would have to assume then either that 1) the hypothesis that continuity of temperament dimensions through stages of growth and development cannot be supported, or that 2) our observations of behavior are not valid measurements of temperament, or that 3) "intervening variables" have occurred between the early observations of behavior and the later observations, which have altered the expected behavior. We know that, in fact, *many* intervening variables have occurred to affect and modify behavior as an individual moves from infancy through the confrontation with his environment at various stages of growth and development. Physiological factors, cognitive development and the process of socialization are among the factors that must be considered as affecting behavior. But it is our position that temperament need not be considered as changed simply because behavior has changed. A person may still feel uncomfortable in new situations even if he has learned to cover this and march smilingly into a room full of strangers. The temperament that was made known in objective observation in early childhood may still be present, though modified by life experiences.

These problems of establishing reliably consistent evidence of the continuity and persistence of dimensions of temperament have caused the issue of change in temperament to remain somewhat murky.

In our work with adults, we do not work on identifying temperament only by making direct observations of behavior but also rely upon the reports of behavior by our adult subjects and upon the meaning which they attach to their behavior in terms of temperament. By inviting the subjects to participate in their own temperamental identification, we are able to include in our evaluations much material that is not directly available to external observation. Using this more subjective method, we have felt that continuity of temperament throughout life stages becomes very apparent although, of course, we see many behavioral variations.

In one of our workshops, we were challenged on this premise of the continuity of temperament by a man who mentioned that his son had shown strong withdrawal when he first entered school. The child would run home from the playground, cry when it was time to go to school, etc. However, his father said, the boy is now in high school and loves school, looks forward to it, and shows no withdrawal. This father looked dubious when we suggested that his son had become adjusted to his school, his friends, and was no longer facing a new situation. Later in the afternoon session, this man remembered that his son had recently come home from his job at a drive-in hamburger spot complaining that "they're getting a new manager and he is going to make lots of changes, there'll be new workers, and I'm going to quit." The father counseled him that if he just gave himself time to live with the new changes a bit he might decide he did not have to quit the job! We think this is quite evidently the current manifestation of this young man's withdrawal response when faced with new situations, as his five-year-old behavior had been. We would predict that he will display a similar reaction as a usual response whenever he meets new situations in his life.

Another young man appeared to us to be slow-to-adapt but was working competently at a troubleshooting job which he enjoyed very much. His job took him into many new situations but his structured way of going to work on the new set of problems was the same. When he first read some of our material, his comment was, "First I want to tell you that you made some mistakes in grammar." Almost every session with him began with such a controlling remark and only as we continued to work with him could he begin to find ways to move into a more comfortable acceptance of our concepts and actually get into group interaction. Interestingly, his mother had saved report cards from his early school years which showed that each year the first quarter's report spoke of his inability to make friends easily and his resistance to following directions. His grades invariably improved over the year and the final report would speak of M.'s complete adjustment after a slow and uncomfortable start. We felt that his particular occupation as troubleshooter was especially suitable for his temperament for it gave him a structured opportunity to begin a new encounter by finding reasons why he could not go along with what he found there!

Sometimes we find that behavior that seems clearly indicative of a particular temperament will appear in an adult in a way which seems quite different from, even opposite to, the temperament stance displayed in the childhood years. Often our patients will say, "I used to be that way but now I've changed," meaning that they no *longer* *act* the same way. Often in our group meetings we ask for volunteers to help us demonstrate our process of identification. Usually, a few people immediately volunteer while others wait to see what's going on. A few will almost stiffen with resistance. We think it would be logical to assume that those who quickly volunteer rank high on the dimension of approach. However, when we talk over with them what their behavior really indicated, we find that some have volunteered because they are being adaptive to group need for volunteers. Others report that they have always been very reluctant to get into new situations, but they regard this attitude as not good and are trying to break out of this natural tendency to hold back. It is like counterphobic behavior in the sense that the individual gets into the behavior that he fears. We consider such people to be withdrawal temperaments even though their *behavior* appears to be the opposite. We think the recognition, "I have always been reluctant, but . . ."

demonstrates that this temperament dimension has been continuous. The same is true for those who told us they had wanted to immediately volunteer but didn't because they had felt it would appear "pushy" or exhibitionistic. These had been words that were often applied to them since they seemed always ready for anything new. Again, we would consider such a statement as indication of a high degree of approach, even though the behavior display had not been outwardly indicative of approach. We have to assume that intervening variables of socialization and cognitive development have worked their effect upon the behavior and that behavior per se does not reflect temperament dimensions in a clear-cut one-to-one way.

We feel that our clinical work with temperament supports the premise that temperament is continuous and persistent. While it is obvious that many influences, both internal and external, have had a part in shaping behavioral responses, it seems that the individual can, with introspection, sort out the overlays of these factors and get to the temperamental dimension that he can identify as definitely his. This is an important point for us since our therapeutic applications of temperament rest upon the idea that we do not expect to work towards changing the temperament dimensions of any individual, but rather feel that acceptance of temperament identity includes the acceptance of temperament as a primary base which the individual brings to the interaction with his environment. It is out of this confrontation of the individual and the environment that behavior is constructed, in our view. This does not preclude change in behavior. In fact, we have discovered that the very process of bringing temperament identity to conscious level can itself influence the construction of changed *behavior* in the individual. New decisions are made, new actions are taken by the individual who has identified and accepted his temperament style as a basic component of his behavior.

IDENTIFYING DIMENSIONS OF TEMPERAMENT

Our first concern, then, is the establishment for each of our patients or clients of a consciousness of *how* he is being himself. Using the nine dimensions of temperament identified in children in the NYLS study, we ask our participants to consider each of the dimensions as a continuum on which they will attempt to project their view of their own behavior. To assist them in this process, we employ the method of constructing Ideal Types which represent the extreme positions on each continuum. For example, we describe behavior which could be considered typical of a very low-active individual and then of a very high-active individual. We ask the client to then attempt to describe how closely he approximates the behavior described in one of the two types on a simple scale of 1 to 5, with a position of 3 representing a neutral or variable estimation of himself on this dimension.

Naturally, we will not find adults behaving in the same way that infants and children do, so it is necessary for us to translate the temperament dimensions established in the earlier study into more appropriate manifestations of the same dimensions in the older age group. The infant observations were in terms of physical manfestations; they did not include any displays of temperament that depended upon ideation. But the behavioral repertoire of older children, adolescents, and adults must take this into account. Thus, our extrapolations to adult behavior include not only physical but mental responses.

We have found that a reading assignment of descriptions of the various Ideal Types and the brief self-rating scale (Appendix A) are helpful tools for the client to use in this process.

This subjective evaluation is primary in our clinical approach since we believe that temperament manifestations can sometimes be (unconsciously) modified or dissembled if the individual has learned that an altered display of himself is more successful in obtaining what he needs from others. In other words, one might repress any display of intensity if such a display had earlier been met with non-acceptance by significant others. Only if the individual is actively engaged in the process of identification of his temperament can he subjectively interpret the meaning of how he acts and reacts to situations. In this way, behavior which might appear to demonstrate a particular temperament position could be misinterpreted by direct observation, which could not get at the subjective meaning of the behavior. This means that we deal with past experiences as something we gave meaning to. We no longer deal with the past except to understand how, in ascribing that meaning, we gave up consciousness of the primary dimensions we were born with. The past history is useful, not in uncovering antecedent causative factors which explain present behavior, but in getting in touch with earlier manifestations of temperament. We encourage the use of childhood records and family anecdotes. Some of our clients have used parents' memory of the child behavior to dig out and get at the ways that temperament was seen in family settings. We are not so concerned with the proven degree of reliability of these admittedly imprecise measures so much as the way these memories and records seem to accord with the client's view of his present-day behavior.

In addition to our emphasis upon the individual's own perceptions of the meaning of his behavior, we work with the group's perceptions of the individual. We have discovered that an individual quickly reveals himself in the process of interaction. In groups in which individuals are well known to each other, for example among the staff of teachers at a private school, or among the social work staff at a social service agency, or in an occupational setting, we find very high agreement in the evaluations that others make of a subject's temperament dimensions. Usually this group opinion closely matches the subject's own evaluation of himself in terms of these dimensions and the process serves to ratify or verify the particular position he has taken on any one dimension. In groups, such as therapy groups where the new member who is attempting to bring his temperament to a more conscious level is not well known to the others, group feedback still plays an important part. Group members who have gone through the process themselves begin to observe evidence of intensity, adaptiveness, and several of the other dimensions quite readily. (Of course, some dimensions such as rhythmicity or distractibility are not quite so visible on short acquaintance.)

Our own experience, as therapists heavily invested in the application of the concept of temperament in adult behavior, has made us aware of cues which may indicate to us the presence of a particular position on a temperament dimension. We make use of this by presenting the information to the subject and asking him how our perceptions of his temperament match up with his own evaluation. Sometimes a client will readily assent to our identification but often he may be startled at such a view of himself if it is at variance with the way he thinks of himself. Often these cues are taken from expressions of what appear to be the opposite of the temperament dimensions we expect. A patient who reports having delayed for a matter of months or years a significant "closing" act (i.e., the final paper necessary for course credit toward graduation; the completion of a bibliography necessary before turning in a dissertation, etc.) is sometimes surprised when we suggest that his temperament seems high on activity. We believe that many people who are very active also have a high degree of anxiety around the successful completion of an activity and will convert their activity into *not* doing the essential completing act, lest they discover that they have failed. As another example, persons may present themselves as self-effacing and may determinedly hold back any strong feelings, sometimes expressing this repression bodily by "holding in" with arms crossed over the chest or even "holding on" to the arms of a chair. They are surprised that we perceive them as having a high level of intensity.

The process of identification of the individual's position on the temperament dimension continua is always seen as tentative, exploratory, and subject to change as we get to know the client better and as he becomes more comfortable with accepting the reality of his temperament at this new level of consciousness. We feel that the individual must establish this knowledge of himself, with all the help that feedback from others can give him, since that individual is the only one who can introspect into the covert meanings of his behavior.

IDENTIFYING STYLE CLUSTERS

It was in clinical observations, also, always with the corroboration of our patients or other participants, that we perceived the regularity with which certain dimensions of temperament occur together. In this sense, then, we believe that certain combinations of temperament dimensions will make up a recognizable *style* of action and/or reaction. We have developed these style clusters in discovering that the wealth of behavioral material that is uncovered in therapy situations emphasizes certain recurring and persistent themes.

The six style designations which we use, Withdrawer, Persister, Adapter, Approacher, Intenser, and Doer, provide a stylistic identification for an individual. Without demanding precise matching of the individual's temperament dimensions to the particular style cluster he seems to most closely approximate, we have found we can now make some predictions and assumptions about the person's interactive experiences. At this point the individual is often surprised to discover that behavior which he had thought of as wrong or sick or in need of therapeutic change is really quite in line with his own inherent style of behavior. The problems which may have brought him for therapy are in fact problems stemming from relationships in which his temperament has not been recognized, accepted and supported.

COMMUNICATING TEMPERAMENT STYLES

After working with an individual to help him become conscious of his temperament style, we are then ready to explore the ways in which the person can communicate this knowledge of himself to others for their support, confirmation and repair. How to arrive at and carry out this communication and deal with subsequent responses represents much of our work with patients and other clients. Many of our patients complain not only about having to become aware of their style, but also about actually communicating this to others for their recognition and response. They experience the latter as placing them in a position vis-à-vis others that is "too vulnerable." Accustomed to manipulating others for the recognition they want, hopeful that others will intuitively know what they need, and fearful of rejection, they resist the idea that open communication of themselves is essential.

We believe that communication of temperament style is the basis of consonant interpersonal relations. Psychologically it forms the base for a healthy self-image and for individual autonomy. In social relationships it becomes the way in which compatible and enduring liaisons may occur. Thus, throughout this book we will emphasize the importance of communication.

This communication can have several crucial effects. As the individual strives for closure, he can use the interactive communication to obtain *recognition* and *confirmation* of his particular style. Secondly, there is the need for *support* which is communicated by actions or reactions of different temperament styles. For example, the

Withdrawer will appear fearful and threatened by change, the Doer will suffer anxiety or "stage fright" before engaging in an activity. Other style clusters will also demonstrate characteristic affective states that indicate needs for supportive interaction. Thirdly, we think that *repair* is an important interactive process for the fullest closure around one's style. Essentially, repair is a response to dissonance which may be experienced as temporarily overwhelming or disabling. When our temperamental direction is stymied, directly or indirectly, this can create distressing feeling states that may have a long-term effect. Essentially, repair involves 1) the participation of a significant other in recognizing and accepting the presence and expression of distress, and 2) the instigation of supportive measures and responses to prepare for further excursions towards closure. If effective repair is missing, there can be crippling effects on the manifestation of style.

RECOGNITION OF TEMPERAMENT STYLES OF OTHERS

The work on communication for confirmation, support, and repair proceeds in group therapy settings, in couples therapy, and in family groups. In these interactive situations, each individual becomes involved not only in the process of identifying and communicating his own temperament but also in learning to recognize the temperament of the others in the group and to respond interactively to others' communication of themselves. In our view of successful and gratifying relationships, the *mutual* recognition and acceptance of temperament is necessary; therefore, identification and communication of self are only half the battle. In each interactive event, in every ongoing relationship, an individual is a receiver as well as a transmitter. To gain skill in recognizing the temperament style of another, often not consciously communicated by the other, and to take that other's style of behavior into account in interacting with him is our aim. It has been our experience that this process is thoughtful, searching and nonthreatening for the most part. In these groups, while emotion-laden material often emerges, we do not work with cathecting emotion, confronting interactions, or behavioral contracts. Our goals are introspective recognition and knowledgeable use of temperament awareness in daily interaction.

Self-identification, communication and recognition of temperament dimensions of significant others are the three primary goals of
the application of these concepts in the adult population. These principles remain in the forefront whether in therapy groups, in marriage or family counseling, or in business or professional applications.

Part II

Identifying Temperament in Adults

5

Temperament as the Inherent Component in Behavior

Every parent with more than one child has recognized that each child comes into the world with ways of reacting that mark that child's individuality. While one may be active and intense, another child might be recognized as being persistent or non-distractible. Not only are these ways of reacting obvious to the observant parent, but they seem to continue as the child grows and develops. In families you will hear remarks like, "Joe was always slow to warm up to anything new," or "Fran's just like Aunt Sally, blows up so easily." The remarkable thing about this rather commonplace observation is that it is so overlooked in much of the thinking that goes on in the effort to construct theories about personality development and interactive behavior.

As long as people have had language so that they could begin to think and reflect about meanings of their own actions and those of others, they have tried to analyze those actions and decide what determines or underlies them. From theories that see individual behavior as determined by the movement of the stars in their galaxies to theories that see behavior as the inevitable response to an external stimulus, we have tried to develop systematic explanations of behavior. For the most part, however, this theory-building has tended to ignore the place that the individual's temperament plays in his behavior. Although temperamental orientations of an individual are

47

not adequate to explain the entire gamut of behavior of any individual, to ignore its presence is to miss understanding the base
upon which that person's behavior is constructed.

Since 1956 the New York Longitudinal Study has been concerned
with the recognition of temperamental traits and the behavioral
consequences of those traits. Starting with a group of newborns, the
New York group first identified the temperament orientations of the
children, then followed the children through the years and observed
the temperamental constellations through the various stages of growth
and development. They have been able to observe the emergence of
emotional disturbance in some of the children, and have linked this
with the dissonance that occurs when parenting has not taken into
account the natural or "given" temperament of the child. They have
been able, by helping parents to recognize, allow, and work with
the natural temperament of their child, to relieve that emotional
distress. They have learned that certain temperamental orientations
have become particularly salient in one person's individuality, that
different traits will be emphasized in another. They have found that
for certain parents children with particular temperaments will be
regarded as "difficult children."

The New York group has been working with these concepts and
carefully measuring and evaluating their findings in terms of parent/
child interaction. However, it is clear that the behavior of these
individuals is expressed in interaction with the "significant others"
in their environment—parents, then teachers, peers, and others who
occupy important roles vis-à-vis the child. And it is in interaction
that the individual is reinforced positively or negatively for his
actions and learns which behavioral consequences of his temperament
will be acceptable and which may be unacceptable to these others.
As a result, an individual may learn to conceal or work against the
natural tendency of his temperament which is apparently troublesome to others (and, of course, to himself, as these others react to
him unfavorably). But he does not really change the basic temperament itself. It is as if one would find that a particular genetic feature
that he had was considered undesirable and thus should be changed,
or at least concealed from others. In our culture, for example, slim
is considered a desirable body build and the person with the more

rounded body structure may suffer through endless efforts to achieve the desired skinny look, or else, in open rebellion and anger, may become unnecessarily obese.

In a similar way, a child might learn that any expression of his high level of intensity was met with evidence that he was creating problems for the parent; without changing the fact of the intensity itself, he could repress, conceal, or perhaps escalate the intensity in response. In such a case, there would be a resulting dissonance between the natural temperamental state and the behavior expressed, often leading to emotional distress. Since expressions of one's temperament begin very early in life and are quite obvious at this early age because they are not yet conditioned or modified, the parents' *responses* to the child's temperament become a part of the "programming" that influences and directs the child's actions, due to the unconscious internalization of these parent messages.

What this means for parenting is clearly obvious in the work of the NYLS. And although the main thrust of their work has been in identifying and studying temperament in as objective a way as possible in order to validate their concepts, it would seem that furtherance of the work might now be in applying these concepts in a broader way.

If parents are to learn to recognize and work with the temperament of their children, it is perhaps the first order of business that they recognize and accept their own temperament and the kind of behavior they construct to deal with or express that temperament. If they are to make use of the knowledge that parent/child interaction will need to take into account the temperaments of both parent and child, they will need to recognize that *all* social interactions of more than superficial depth or duration will be based, at least in part, upon the temperaments of the individuals involved. Thus, any relationship that involves the individual in more than simply contractual exchange will deal not only with the communication that goes on between the parties in the relationship but with the underlying temperaments of the parties in this relationship.

It is for this reason that we have extended the concepts of temperament as developed by the New York study into a more direct concern with temperament as seen in the adult population. Our concern is not only in the interests of parents interacting with their children's temperaments but also in adults interacting with others in their network of social systems, in their marriages or other intimate relationships, in their occupational systems, and in any other social system in which they find themselves.

Temperament can be seen as an individual's orientation or "set" in respect to several different traits or dimensions. There is probably no exhaustive or completely discriminating list of traits that could perfectly encompass all variations of temperament. Some students of temperament have used introversion-extroversion as a temperament orientation. Others have spoken of "ascendency," or tendency toward dominance or leadership, as a temperament orientation. The list which we have chosen to work is the list used in the work with children. These traits are primarily ways of acting and reacting which can be manifested in some physical way in infants, before they have learned to express themselves in language. Thus they do not deal with the *concepts* of "leadership" or on "introversion-extroversion." These ways of reacting represent a "style" or manner of reacting and are not meant to describe the behavior itself; rather they describe the way any behavior is expressed. In a sense it is an adverb to describe the verb of what is being done. One goes to a party —eagerly, or reluctantly, or in high spirits, etc.

It is our conclusion, based upon our work with adults, that these temperamental traits, which can be discerned and identified in the very young child, remain a part of the person throughout his life. This is not to say that they are unchanging, for that would be to deny the fact that maturation has any effect. Again, without insisting that temperament is a genetic factor, we can draw an analogy to the individual who is born with genetic determination of white skin. As he lives in the environment and grows from infancy to adulthood, the skin may darken and coarsen or become lined with the effects of the experiences he has lived through. It is still recognizable as white skin. In such a way, the same temperament may be expressed in a different way as an adult than as a child and the early identification which can be made by observing the child before he develops language facility will not "change" but will develop through ideation and become manifest in a somewhat different fashion.

For example, the trait of activity level which is seen in infants as marked by the degree of motor activity, might persist in an adult as an orientation to action in the sense of problem solving. The adult manifestation of the "high activity" trait would be a tendency toward mastery by actively doing something about any situation. When finding himself in a new group, for example, such a person might immediately begin to find out what he needed to do, while the person of low activity level might react by simply waiting for something to happen or might engage in observing his surroundings without forming strategies of action. In dealing with temperament on the adult level, it is important to translate the early evidence of the individual's temperament into adult behavior. In the following chapter we will describe the content of the nine dimensions of temperament, both as they are seen by the earlier study and as we find them in the older population.

Interaction or interpersonal behavior is the arena in which temperament makes itself known. Even though one's temperament is a part of one's own individuality, it is in the exchanges with others in our social spheres that it is expressed. Every transaction then carries not only a communication of meaning but also a communication of the individual's feeling about the exchange. These messages about our temperament create a response in the partner to the transaction. If we see these temperamental ways of reacting as really a "given" in the individual and not simply learned in socialization or by conditioning, then we will accept and value a person's particular orientation as a part of that individual, both in ourselves and in others. However, it is also evident that certain ways of reacting may be valued more in some situations or by some people and thus create the feeling that some particular reactivity may be wrong or not acceptable. By overvaluing achievement, for example, we may impart to the person who has a temperament marked by a low level of activity that he is inferior. If one is of an easygoing, low-key temperament, one might respond negatively to intensity or one might respond negatively to intensity if it is accompanied with a message of disagreement or challenge. It might not be the disagreement or challenge that could be difficult for someone to deal with, but the fact that the message was delivered so hotly by the intense person.

It is our belief, then, that temperament recognition, acceptance, and communication can become the basis for the productive expression of one's autonomy. In addition, the ability to recognize and accept the temperament of others with whom one is in interpersonal action is to be able to respond to the autonomy of others and to release ourselves from the impossible task of taking responsibility for others' thoughts or actions. In later chapters we will take up the subject of temperaments in interaction. But before we deal with temperament in others, it is important to learn to recognize our own ways of reacting and to gain insight into the ways we express our temperamental stance in our daily life.

6

Nine Dimensions of Temperament

There are several components to the temperament system of an individual and it might even be possible to pinpoint where an individual stands on all of the nine temperament traits that Chess and Thomas identified in their work with young children. It is more likely that only a few of the nine dimensions are particularly important in any one individual. An individual might arrive at one or two outstanding temperamental characteristics with a few others as parts of a basic pattern. Others of the traits may not seem important or definite to the person who is trying to come to some understanding of his temperament and may be relatively ignored.

In attempting to extend the work that has been done in identifying the important temperamental traits for children to an application of these concepts in adults, it is necessary to extend the meanings of the particular traits from the pre-language evidence in young children to the more sophisticated conceptualization of the adult. Rather than relying upon the observable behavior and making inferences from this observed behavior to the temperamental position which it manifests, we can now deal with the verbal reports of the individual and his thinking about the meaning of his behavior, as manifesting a temperamental stance. This has both the advantage of involving the individual in his own evaluation of his behavior (thus allowing confirmation or modification of an observer's interpretation) and the disadvantage of inviting the less objective interpretation of the subject. In such a method, the potential for the subject to simply indulge in what he judges an acceptable "presentation of self" may distort the true picture of the individual's temperament. However, if the person can be convinced of the acceptability of any or all temperamental positions and that no position is more desirable than any other, the bias towards an interpretation other than what feels natural for him can be minimized.

Although the position of an individual in terms of any one of these temperamental traits might be thought of as a particular location on a continuum, it is difficult to describe with any degree of exactness what that particular position on the continuum means. A better method of helping an individual locate himself in regard to a particular trait consists of creating opposing Ideal Types as presenting the extreme position on the continuum and asking the subject to compare his own interpretation of his temperament to these Ideal Types and to indicate how closely he approximates one or the other of the two Types.

The nine traits which we are using are direct extrapolations of the nine traits which were used in the child group studied in the New York Longitudinal Study of human behavior. Building on the conclusions of our study as to the persistence of temperamental characteristics throughout adult development stages, we believe that the adult manifestations of temperament will be continuations of the childhood positions. Therefore, to introduce other dimensions of temperament in an adult study would confuse the issue of persistence of temperament. If new traits were discernible in adults which were not identifiable in children, we would have to attempt to answer the question of when or under what circumstances such a trait entered the picture of the individual's temperament.

1. ACTIVITY LEVEL

The trait of *activity level,* as identified in the study of children, "describes the level, tempo, and frequency with which a motor component is present in the child's functioning" (1, p. 20). A high level is not difficult to discern even in the very young child who spends his waking hours in exploring, reaching and moving; if held on the lap, he jumps, thrashes his arms about and, if not clutched, will bounce off his parent's lap. This activity is usually regarded positively in our culture and we tend to restrict the child as little as possible, perhaps even to encourage or reward this activity. The child with low level of activity will lie or sleep quietly, may not seem as eager to learn to walk or move about. In societies which practice swaddling of infants, the child who is temperamentally very active will not be rewarded or encouraged.

As the individual grows and develops, this active exploratory activity may became manifested in mental as well as physical activity and be evidenced in approaching any situation by engaging in some sort of action. A new environment engages this person in planning and carrying out some action strategies of his own in the situation. A problem is seen in terms of what shall be done to reach a solution, a piece of art or a musical composition in terms of how it was put together or how one would go about painting or performing it. It is probable that the highly active person will become restive, may even go to sleep, at quiet, spectator types of events and will get some relief from this inactivity if he can engage in some problem-solving thinking about it. The highly active person watches a sports event on TV, if he watches TV, by sometimes verbally playing the game himself, even leaning over to catch a pass being thrown on the screen. We find that when brought into a new group or introduced to a new protocol for group participation, the high level of activity person will immediately want to establish how he is to act, will perhaps undertake to give suggestions or objections or opinions about the project.

The person with low level of activity temperament is, of course, more likely to react to a new situation with much less emphasis upon his own actions in it. He or she may tend to observe, contemplate, speculate about meanings, get in touch with the totality of the event, and in other ways think about rather than act in response to whatever situation he finds himself in. This person will more likely not present his own plan or venture an opinion when new group situations are presented, but will remain as much as possible in an observer stance and will not feel constrained to determine his strategy or make some evidence of his feelings known to the group. In viewing a piece of art or hearing a musical composition, he will more likely quietly get in touch with the meaning for himself of the artist's projection, with little thought of how he would or could have done it. He may in fact be better as a *critic* of art in its many forms than as a performer or practitioner of the arts.

2. RHYTHMICITY

In children, the identification of this category in the NYLS was based on the "degree of rhythmicity or regularity of repetitive biological functions" (1, p. 20). Those children with regular or rhythmic responses could be counted on to eat, sleep, have active periods at predictable times, with, of course, some deviations from those expected times. The irregular children, on the other hand, did not develop patterns of activity, but ate, slept, and played in a highly unpredictable fashion.

In adults, this tendency for regularity might be manifested in routinization, even to the point of ritualization of behavior. The person with regular temperament might discover an optimum way to go to work and then not vary this established way, except, of course, for some necessary exception. Such an individual might sense uneasiness or frustration when faced with a move to new quarters or into a new situation. Rearranging one's belongings in a new home disturbs the sense of orderliness and "everything in its place" that is pleasing to the regular person; restlessness and distress may continue until the new situation is routinized and has become familiar. It may also be that the "regular" person is more tuned in to bodily rhythms and may be aware of hunger at certain times, periods of low energy in mid-afternoon, or the imminence of the menstrual period in a woman. Real discomfort will be experienced if the regular person is prevented from the orderly routine of his life, though he is able to deviate when interruptions occur and then later recover and reestablish the patterns.

The person who is of irregular temperament may operate without apparent patterns or routines and may find himself feeling very constrained by the schedule that is "tight" and repetitive. This person is hard to fit into a daily or weekly activity as he will find many reasons not to be able to make the scheduled activity, to be late in arriving, or to "forget" the activity entirely. The belongings, and sometimes even the personal appearance, of the irregular person may be in some state of disarray, in which the irregular person moves easily, plucking what he needs out of a desk covered with papers or wearing "uncoordinated" outfits with carefree dash and elan. Irregular persons tend not to be aware of bodily needs and may work until exhausted or eat at odd times and with little sense of the set schedules of those around them.

3. APPROACH OR WITHDRAWAL

This temperament trait describes the initial reaction that a person makes to a new situation or even a new acquaintance. Those children who were seen as being "at home" wherever they were, or comfortable with persons new to them, were seen as approach temperaments. Children who demonstrated their resistance to new stimuli were considered withdrawal temperaments.

In adults, we find the approach person welcoming new experiences and feeling at ease with strangers, even to the point of being somewhat gullible. This person rarely thinks of long-term consequences, but jumps into a new situation with alacrity. Often, after he has gotten into the situation, he finds that he is somewhat surprised and disheartened to find himself again in a spot that is not working out to his advantage and wishes that he had been more cautious and had stopped to evaluate consequences. On the other hand, he also experiences much that more cautious persons never dare to get into and has many and varied friends, and these advantages are important to him. When his adventures turn out badly, he finds himself mystified and resentful and probably makes those "never again" resolves, only to forget them when the next stimulus occurs.

The withdrawal temperament person is found sitting on one side of the room where friends are gathered at a party and needs gentle prodding to get into the spirit of the evening. Faced with new situations, he initially retreats, acts bored, has other more pressing affairs to take care of. He probably does not actually refuse to go along, but just feels reluctance at a change that strikes him as too peremptory.

Left to his own devices, without some encouragement by caring others, he may find that he allows too many opportunities for new experiences to pass him by. Given understanding and encouragement, he is often a most active and energetic participant when he finally overcomes his withdrawal.

4. ADAPTABILITY

This trait, concerned not with initial reactions but with the subsequent ability to modify one's actions to fit the expectations or wishes of others, is discerned in children by readiness (or resistance) to show conforming behavior to parental pressures.

As an adult, the adaptive person will find himself studying the situation to identify what the expected behavior is so that he can become a part of it. He takes on the mood and affect of others and, in playing a role, "becomes" that role. The adaptive partygoer is soon the life of the party. The adaptive college student may be Joe College himself by midpoint of his freshman year. One adaptive individual described herself as having a different self-identity with each of several friends. Such a person can get hooked into the mood of others for reasons that she doesn't understand and may feel a certain uneasiness until she has been able to pick up some cues from others to form a basis for her own behavior. This is one trait which may be overvalued by our mass society. The person who is persuaded easily to accept the norms of the group does not risk the subtle disapproval of that group which might consider him eccentric at best, and a deviant in cases of more serious failures to adapt.

The non-adaptive individual will not readily change his own position to conform to group or individual pressures. He is impervious to norms and prefers to operate in terms of self-evaluation of the circumstances. He may appear somewhat "cool" in the sense of being unresponsive to group pressures to conform and at times seems aloof and disinterested. However, his contribution is likely to be valuable in the sense of introducing alternatives and new directions. Every ongoing group can use the talents of the non-adapters even though they may not seem to "work well" in terms of group process.

This particular trait is rather hard to identify in our culture with its demands for conformity. Most of us have experienced demands for adapting to the pressures of group living and most of us have felt at times that such demands were overbearing. So, knowing that we have done our share of conforming, we jump to the conclusion that we are adapters. Then, remembering our discomfort and, on occasion, resentment at these pressures, we decide we are non-adapters. So it takes patient introspection to get in touch with the particular stance on this temperamental trait that feels right with the individual. Generally, if one can quickly and easily "get into the role" of another and experience this role as one's own, much as an actor "becomes" the role he is acting, one is near the "adaptive" end of the continuum. If one senses the pressures to adapt as the loss of one's own autonomy and as an uncomfortable demand, one is more nearly non-adaptive.

5. INTENSITY

This temperament trait has to do with the strength of the response to any stimulus, either a positive or a negative response. The child is observed as to the amount of energy he puts into his response and is seen as intense if his response shows a high degree of investment of attention and activity.

This high intensity person is likely to seem mercurial as he is intensely joyful at one time, intensely morose at another, but both represent a way of responding that is expressed dramatically. It is as if the intense person is communicating in the broad and exaggerated gestures of the stage and his point of view is not so much expressed as it is driven home with forcefulness. "Always" and "never" are common words with the high intensity person, as in "You are *always* late for dinner," or "I will *never* go there again." It may also seem to the intense person that he is very powerful since he is aware of expending a great deal of energy. This person may feel that he personally *makes* people feel happy or angry or whatever and, since at early ages parents are likely to try to "calm down" high intensity crying, boisterous playfulness, or the "tantrums" that occur when the child is frustrated, the intense person may come to feel that he overwhelms people and that he must try to keep his feelings down. As adults these people feel that others can never understand them and may resent the constant feeling that they can't communicate with ordinary people. They both yearn for communication with another intense person and feel some alarm when another person *does* express intense feelings, feeling that they have *caused* this. People who are of fairly low intensity are often strongly attracted to the high intensity person, especially to their positive feelings of enthusiasm and excitement, from which they can get vicarious excitement.

The person who is low in intensity of expression is certainly not a person without strong feelings and convictions. It is just that his expression is more measured and contained. He is probably not known for his charisma and is rather appreciated for his ability to keep things on an even keel in situations in which people with high intensity can stir up a hornet's nest of feelings. He is a good listener usually and in many cases appears to be the strong silent type. This person, even while quietly enjoying a more intense companion, is somewhat mystified and puzzled by what seems overreactive behavior. He needs help sometimes in simply accepting highly intense reactions without coming on in heavy "adult" squelching of the other person, or in defensive feelings of "What have *I* done to cause all this!"

6. THRESHOLD OF RESPONSIVENESS

This dimension refers to how intense the stimulus in the environment must be before the individual will respond. If the child does not seem responsive to or did not seem to notice new surroundings or discern the difference between old and familiar and new and strange stimuli, he is rated as having a high threshold. If he is immediately aware (and regardless of whether his awareness is marked with curiosity, fear, avoidance, or other responses), he is judged to have a low threshold of responsiveness.

In adults, we believe that low threshold may make itself known as impulsiveness as the individual picks up on cues, perhaps earlier than others, and responds to those cues. If the low threshold is accompanied in an individual's temperament with high intensity, the person may appear to be highly "charged" and, to one who doesn't recognize the temperament traits, quite unpredictable and difficult to deal with. The person who is highly sensitive to the "mood" of a place and has an immediate response to the "romantic" setting of "candlelight and wine" or the noisy bistro is expressing his low threshold of responsiveness.

The high threshold person will simply not "pay attention" to changes in the environment unless they become quite escalated in strength, and this person may also appear to treat people with a certain bland sameness, as if he does not recognize the differences in people. Other people's reactions are not quickly apparent and his response when asked what went on in a situation is, "I didn't notice," or "I never thought of that." The high threshold individual will be likely to have quite a bit to respond to when stimuli build up enough to cause him to respond, so his response may be somewhat explosive and pervasive when it does finally occur. It is as if he suddenly becomes aware of many things having piled up, and he discharges all of his feelings at once.

7. QUALITY OF MOOD

It is observed that in some infants there is a certain contented enjoyment of surroundings and much cooing and pleasant behavior, while others do much fussing and crying. Adults, of course, do not fuss and cry in the infantile way, but negative quality of mood is a temperament trait of one who is somewhat worrisome and disinclined to look on the bright side. A certain pessimism of mood is marked by a fairly serious and unjovial demeanor. This is not without its relieving sense of humor and some of the most ironic and pungent wit is delivered with the "deadpan" and unsmiling manner of the comic with the negative quality of mood. This person may err on the side of refusing to recognize encouraging or promising developments. He may also work too hard since he never really believes that things are going to reach a rewarding state of accomplishment. He does, of course, have a sense of enjoyment, but it seems to be very selective and only emerges when everything is going well.

The person with a high quality of mood finds something to laugh about and enjoy in himself and his environment. Such a person is a joy to be around as his infectious good humor and exuberance brighten the day and lighten the load. He may err in evaluating his surroundings too optimistically and may not recognize that things are not always as bright as he would like to believe. He may, in fact, make a joke, laugh things off and otherwise use his quality of mood in response to difficult situations, and sometimes needs help in recognizing that he is making light of problems rather than dealing with them realistically. He is global in his capacity to enjoy, and only if things are really going badly will he lose this capacity.

8. DISTRACTIBILITY

The individual who is distractible is, of course, one who, while engaged in one activity, is easily switched to another. The person who is engaged in a conversation and suddenly begins to become engrossed in a radio announcement from the next room can leave his less distractible companion talking to the wall. The person who begins to work at one task may never get it done without side trips, fantasy interludes, or other interruptions, not because he is obtuse, obstructionist or absentminded, but simply because he is easily distracted. This trait is sometimes a difficult one for others to tolerate. Parents of a distractible child have to fight down exasperation as their child does not seem to stick to his tasks or fulfill their expectations for promptness. Spouses or other intimate friends may entertain feelings of being discounted as the distractible person sometimes forgets his obligations to them in pursuit of some fresh interest. On the other hand, this person can be a constant source of new interests and fresh directions if his distractibility can be recognized and valued.

The non-distractible person is rarely seen as unreliable in the sense of neglecting or forgetting his objectives. He can follow a task to its completion without turning his interest to other activities and will ignore the stimulus from the environment.

9. PERSISTENCE

High persistence is seen as the tendency to continue an activity in the face of obstacles, in addition to the tendency to keep on with a task for a considerable span of time. In adults we often find persistent people running a subject "into the ground" by continuing to dwell upon it, enlarge on it, explain it and otherwise indulge in overkill. Not only does the highly persistent person continue an activity overlong, but he often finds himself annoyed and frustrated if attempts are made to interrupt him or deflect his interest to another focus. It is as if he fails to pick up cues from others as to when they have understood him or have "had enough." High persistence, seen as perseverance, is a much admired trait and leads often to accomplishing what might have looked to others like an impossible task. Some of our best scientific discoveries have been made by those who have "refused to give up" and whose persistence earned them the glory of eventual success.

The person with low persistence will not display this dogged determination but will have an attention span that is not maintained until a task has been done down to dotting the last "i" or crossing the last "t". Also, this type of person will not be so invested in his activity that he rejects any attempts to interrupt—he may even welcome an interruption.

The Ideal Types constructed here are meant only as stereotypical descriptions. No person will fit any descriptions *exactly,* but the picture drawn provides a reasonable abstraction of the meaning of the extreme positions on these continuums.

REFERENCE

1. THOMAS, A., CHESS, S., and BIRCH, H. G. *Temperament and Behavior Disorders in Children.* New York: New York University Press, 1968.

7

Style Clusters:

From Child to Adult

In previous chapters, we have dealt with the nine dimensions of temperament which we have used (following the work with children in the New York Longitudinal Study), as if they were each discrete dimensions upon which one could settle on a meaningful position or score. Temperament could then be seen as a profile of scores on the dimensions, and behavior as predictably based upon such profiles. Actually, in clinical observations and in non-clinical applications of our principles, we have found that certain tendencies often seem to occur together and from this information we have been able to set up some descriptions of various *styles* of behavior by which we can usefully draw some conclusions as to how people may perform under various situations.

On the other hand, these style clusters are not nearly so exact (perhaps one should say not *even* so exact) as what is often referred to as a "syndrome" of physical manifestations by which certain illnesses come to be recognized so that certain expectations as to the course of that illness can be taken into account. However, the analogy is useful and the value of thinking of temperament in terms of styles of behavior which can be seen as logically whole can have predictive use as we try to understand our own and others' behavior. However, we do not wish to label persons as belonging to certain style clusters

64

and then, having applied the label, construct our own behavior toward people in terms of the label we have given them. Setting up categories of behavior often results in a therapist and other persons establishing a mode for treating or behaving towards people so categorized. Our objective is rather to provide the individual with a way to think about his temperament as his individual style. In making decisions about how he wants to make use of his conscious knowledge of himself as having an inherent temperament, he can use his recognition of his style cluster in interacting with others.

CONSTELLATIONS OF TEMPERAMENT TRAITS IN CHILDREN

In earlier work with temperament in children, the New York group described several such types of temperament and gave rough estimates as to the proportion of their sample which fell within the various types. They were able to identify three constellations of temperament traits that occurred often enough to be predictive of certain kinds of behavior. The labels that were given to these groups were, understandably, given from the perspective of the adults who were observing the children. They found that about 40 percent of the children observed were so-called Easy Children, which is to say easy for parents, teachers, and others to deal with. Another 10 percent were called Difficult Children since they did not show a willing compliance or conformity to the expectations of parents and other caretakers. Still another 15 percent were labeled Slow-to-warm-up Children who were somewhere in between the other two types in terms of readiness and acceptance of the socialization process. Even so, this accounts for only 65 percent of the sample, so we conclude that the other 35 percent were not so easily identified as belonging to a particular grouping but had other combinations of temperament dimensions. And, of course, with those who were included in the categories of Easy, Difficult, or Slow-to-warm-up Children, there were many individual situational variations. Few of the Difficult Children were thought "difficult" under all situations. Certain children were slower-to-warm up under some conditions, not as slow under certain other conditions. Categorization is simply a tool which is available to help understand the temperament base of many behaviors.

Because the assessment of the children's behavior was made from the viewpoint of parents and other adults in the Thomas/Chess studies, naturally they were not getting the child's own subjective evaluation of his behavior. We can imagine, for example, that a child who was very persistent and highly irregular in his behavior, and was *allowed* to behave in this manner with complete approval of his parents, might be very surprised that he was part of a group labeled Difficult Children! For illustrative purposes, we would like to briefly review the childhood temperament constellations that were identified in the study of children before going on to describe some of the somewhat parallel style clusters that we have observed in adults.

Easy Children, that 40 percent of the Thomas/Chess study who were seen as "easy" to deal with by parents and observers, were said to be quite regular or predictable, quick to adapt to new demands or situations to which they were introduced, with a generally positive quality of mood and only mild or moderate intensity. It is understandable to any parent that the child who can be counted on to eat, sleep, and play at predictable times, who will need only minimal exposure to new people or new situations such as going to school, visiting friends, etc., in order to be comfortable, can be a joy to be around. If the child also is generally happy and contented and is not given to vigorous or intense expression of his wishes, the parent can probably proudly say, "That child never gives me a moment's worry. Such a good child." Whether such a temperament constellation, thoroughly approved and reinforced in childhood, is a constellation that makes life "easy" in a highly competitive adult society, which is more likely to reward productivity than pleasantness, is another question.

The Difficult Child of the earlier study was seen as one with a constellation of irregularity, a tendency to withdraw from new situations and to remain uncomfortable (slow to adapt) even after numerous exposures, to have a fairly low, discontented mood, and to be very intense in expression of himself. Such a child has caused many a parent to seek the child psychiatrist. He has, perhaps, become the victim of complete exasperation or even of child abuse at the hands of his parents and other caretakers. These individuals may become intense achievers as adults and may become perfectly comfortable with themselves. Such a person will probably never become one who easily "wins friends and influences people" (nor does he care to).

The Slow-to-warm-up Child, who represented about 15 percent of the sample of children, was described as being fairly slow to adapt to new situations but with less intensity and more regularity than the Difficult Children. It was felt that these children, if allowed a slower pace of meeting change, often became interested and involved participants. We can imagine these people as adults being seen as the most stable group in society, not rushing headlong into new changes but being steady, positive participants once they become involved. Even so, we could envision that the Slow-to-warm-up Child, if pressured for quick action, might also become increasingly resistant and become more involved in protecting his right to not adapt, thus delaying further his ability to move ahead.

It seems we can see these groupings of temperament traits somewhat like blood types. There is a type of blood, Type O, which is known as the "universal donor" which every receiver will be able to accept. We might think of the Easy Child constellation as being that type of child whom almost every adult would find acceptable. Then blood Type B, the type which all other types except other Type Bs reject, would be analogous to the Difficult Child whom all but a very few adults would find difficult to deal with. However, between these two extremes we find many children whom some parents and adults would find very appealing, attractive and, thus, easy for them to deal with while other parents would find these same children too "noisy," or too "stubborn," or too "lazy," etc. These judgments would have as much to say about parents and their particular temperaments as about the children themselves. For example, a child who is very intense and with a low threshold of responsiveness is regarded by some as peppy, cute, full of life. The same child, or another with these same temperament traits, could be viewed by her parents as boisterous, exhausting, and very tiring and tiresome. It is also true that this same very intense child who is positively accepted in childhood roles and reinforced for manifesting this behavior might find at another period of life that these same traits were regarded as inappropriate or unwelcome and feel herself discounted for being the same essential person who was earlier admired. A woman who was popular, admired, and lively in courtship days finds that in the role of mother, with its subordination of her needs to those of husband and children, intensity becomes manifested in "demandingness" and low threshold of response becomes "flying off the handle."

So we surmise that temperament traits can manifest themselves in different ways under differing conditions and will also be responded to differently by persons with differing temperaments. It is easy to see that studies of temperament are not going to lead to simple formulas for dealing effectively with life situations. The goal is rather to recognize the temperament base of behavior so that we can be aware of its influence in our ongoing life situation.

As we have reviewed the three temperament constellations identified and quantified in the sample of children, we have become aware of the many behavioral situations in which temperament plays a part. In adults, where different goals are to be met and where the individual is involved in a much wider scope of life situations, the temperament traits of childhood to which family and school acquaintances responded will now meet many new exigencies. Under these circumstances, adult styles of behavior become recognizable in individuals and provide an operational tool which assists the individual in a conscious identification of his temperament.

8

The Non-Adaptive Child
Grows Up

In view of our observations that temperament traits persist in individuals into adult stages, we would expect that the childhood clusters would persist and that Easy Children would grow up into Easy Adults, and so forth. This seems to be only partially true because the requirements and expectations that surround people as they move through the different stages of adulthood impinge in varying ways upon the individual. The more recent thinking of personality development as being a lifelong process with different expectations at different ages consequently demands different responses of us as we move through life stages. We have postulated that the temperament of the individual persists but that the behavior that emerges is sometimes responded to by others quite differently in adulthood.

It has become apparent to us in our clinical observations that the temperament dimension of adaptability is crucial in the occurrence of interpersonal dissonance and in producing emotional dis-ease. Just as we learned that a child who seemed to show the constellation of temperament dimensions known as the Difficult Child was more likely to need psychiatric intervention, so we find that those who show style clusters in which slowness to adapt is present are likely to have interpersonal difficulties as adults. This appears to be a logical outcome since this trait will be evidenced by resistance to pressures from others to abandon a personal stance and go along with external demands. To be slow to adapt is to be generally resistant to the pressures of others and to obstruct, divert, or at least slow down any compliance to others. In adults we have found that two of the six style clusters we have identified include a slow-to-adapt component. The Withdrawer appears to behave in a way that will control and sometimes coerce others so that he can hang on to his non-adaptive position. The Persister maintains his slow-to-adapt stance by warding off or ignoring any input from others.

THE WITHDRAWER

The Slow-to-warm-up Child, who was seen in the earlier study as one with some withdrawal and slow adaptability, as well as a fairly low level of activity, would present a picture of a person who tended to resist change. Mercifully, this temperament cluster usually included mild intensity so that efforts to move the child forward probably did not become pitched battles and the child finally moved ahead. These same traits, seen in the adult, will present a picture of some stability, as mentioned earlier, but also may disadvantage this person in a fast-paced and fast-changing society.

This style cluster results in behavior that can become dull, boring, routine, and lacking in stimulation. The Withdrawer seldom greets a new suggestion for activity with any enthusiasm and is much more likely to find a reason why his participation is not possible. Oftentimes the reason is projected onto the activity suggested: "No, it's not a good movie." "No, the people at that party will not be people I want to be with." If persuaded to go along, the Withdrawer will often spend most of the evening at the party watching the social interaction; however, if allowed the time to warm up, he can become involved.

One of our favorite Withdrawers grabbed an interesting book and sat in an adjacent room at our house one evening. On another occasion with a much smaller gathering, he was pleasant but did not contribute much until fairly late in the evening when he finally, having worked past his tendency for withdrawal, told us in quiet tones but with a good deal of enthusiasm of some work he was doing and became the center of an animated discussion. In the business world, a Withdrawer, in spite of valuable contributions, will not seek nor welcome changes, even promotions. If the change or new method is imposed peremptorily, the Withdrawer will feel real discomfort and resentment which make for difficult interactions and may result in open conflict. Certainly, this style seems to delay growth and development. The issue here seems to be centered around the need for control on the part of the Withdrawer. The recognition of this tendency to maintain control is the key to communication.

The Withdrawer, as he encounters new expectations or new situations, develops strategies to keep from moving ahead before he is ready. His temperament is expressed in ways which will allow him to keep control of the situation to prevent his having to adapt too rapidly. In groups we have seen Withdrawers control the situation by simply refusing to be part of the group activity, by complaining that the new group plan is impractical, untried and not well thought through. In one-to-one interactions, these "controllers" set up rules to provide themselves room to withdraw: "Alright, we'll go to the party, but we're coming home at 9:30." "Give me proof that our 16-year-old won't bring the car back a wreck."

They seem to have an unerring sense of the correct way to behave in various situations and the correct procedures to carry out. The Withdrawer will pay minute attention to role requirements. Men, carrying out what they think are the traditional requisites of masculinity, are the authoritative heads of the house; they control the money; they determine the family values and activities; they are in charge of discipline and punishment for those who do not comply with their demands. Women Withdrawers may also behave in this manner though their disciplinary and punishing measures may employ guilt.

In their cognitive style as well, the Withdrawers display a strongly oppositional stance. They seem to learn by first looking for something that is not correct or can be seen as wrong. This seems to produce an initial alienated position that can be cleared up only by continuing the interaction to a point of understanding. Then the Withdrawer can feel included. It is rewarding to see a Withdrawer finally see the light and say, "I never looked at it that way before."

The questioning from a Withdrawer can be dogged but it may also be stimulating because it often opens up areas not previously considered. On the other hand, being grilled by a Withdrawer is sometimes like a courtroom experience with a predetermined verdict of guilty.

Once Withdrawers achieve some familiarity with new situations, they can enter in fully and enjoy themselves, although they like to stay generally with the familiar.

In cases where this temperament style has been suppressed or unrecognized in childhood, or where present adult demands for change are very pressing, the resulting dissonance (a conflict between the natural temperament and the environmental pressures) can produce real emotional distress.

If their early tendency to withdraw is reacted to with harsh rejection, or without recognizing their need for support toward social situations, this may lead to the development of a frightened, seriously withdrawn individual who is substantially alienated from others and even from himself. This person often desperately does not want others to let him carry out his withdrawal, but he cannot admit his fears and ask for help. It was particularly moving listening to a patient describe how he sat alone in his car for four hours hoping someone in his family would return and ask him to join them in an activity he had declined. We would say that this dissonance was around his need for support, his inability to ask for it, his family's inability to recognize it.

The Withdrawer who is suffering from dissonance often sees the world as noxious, un-understanding, and alienating and he will respond by developing over-controlling behavior towards those around him. Instead of seeking understanding, he will control his fear of rejection by compelling others to go along with him, often by injunctions, sometimes even by physical coercion. His argumentativeness is experienced as controlling rather than information seeking. He will have a strong tendency to fall back on accusations of unfairness and disappointment. The victims find themselves desperately trying to become understood by the Withdrawer who now seems to have the upper hand. Frequently the spouse or other intimate associate of the Withdrawer is controlled in ways that are designed to denigrate her and she may have difficulty freeing herself from a situation which is severely punitive.

Following are case studies of Withdrawers who have shown some evidence of dissonance and who have come to us with some interactive difficulties. Cases in which pathological manifestations and interpersonal alienation are more severe will appear in later chapters.

Case of R.R.

This young married woman shows marked propensity to overuse the withdrawal component of her style cluster. The withdrawal tendency appears to be a response of scared feelings and anxiety, often experienced around some excitement. Excitement is feared, and she wants to move away from it before it becomes overwhelming and destructive. Control then becomes the central striving in relationships. The unstated position is something like, "If I can control you (object), you will not leave me, surprise me, put me in some new and overwhelming position." Her attempt is to maintain familiar patterns, for adventures into new experiences bring on anxiety again. This leads to setting up a scheduled, highly structured life. She complains that life is boring and indeed appears to have a negative quality of mood and a rather sour expectation, leaning heavily toward pessimism. Her attempt to alter this mood results in a cramped, fixed, almost inappropriate smile. The smile is meant to ward off the production of any excitement, particularly of a negative nature, an argument, perhaps. Her relationships are difficult because she can really trust no one. Sexual experiences are also something to be withdrawn from so as to avoid both the excitement of orgasm and the stimulation of actually entering into the experience very often. We have worked with R. to recognize that excitement is available to her and is a positive experience towards which she can move with interactive help. We want R. to be able to communicate to her husband that she recognizes her tendency to withdraw and that she does need time to move toward new experiences of exciting possibilities. We think she may need also to communicate this at work so that her supervisor may make use of her considerable talents at organizing and setting up useful routines. If she is allowed to remain in positions where her control is never challenged, she can become bored, rigid, and sour.

Case of J.R.

This 30-year-old man was seen in one of our groups and displayed a style cluster which we identified as that of the Withdrawer. Although he had completed his A.B. degree, he was employed in a routine assembly line job at an automobile plant. He reported he was dissatisfied with his job because he felt it did not use his skills, and was dissatisfied with his life which was organized around this unstimulating job. Working on the night shift made his marriage unsatisfactory. (His wife worked as a teacher during the day.) However, he was unable to extricate himself. He reported that he did not know in what occupational direction he wanted to move, although his most satisfactory earlier work had been in casework with adolescents and his undergraduate degree was in psychology. He felt "tonguetied," he said, whenever he was interviewed for a possible job, even when requesting a small change in his assembly line job.

In the group, J.R. was pleasant but usually quiet, although he eventually began to bring some interesting observations to others. The group began to insist that he take some positive and direct steps and were happy for him when he could report that he had looked into graduate programs in his field. He was gratified by their interest, but, in fact, felt diffident about accepting their support. "I should not need to depend on others. I should be able to be self-starting enough to decide what I need to do and do it myself," he said, with embarrassment. Like many men, he viewed dependency on others, even for support and encouragement, as weakness. He had been refusing the help that others were only too ready to give him once they realized his need for them.

We think he would have continued his tendency to withdraw if there had been no communication with others. His withdrawal, accompanied by his low intensity of expression, made his friends unaware that he was even unhappy, and his slow adaptability made him fearful of any rather large change in life style and life direction.

On Being a Withdrawer: Positive and Negative Aspects

The Withdrawer who is able to recognize and accept the reality of this style may deal with this knowledge of himself in several ways. On the positive side, he can realize that his more cautious approach to new situations is valuable for many reasons: not all changes are

positive so he may play a role in making a "cool" evaluation necessary; old friends and old familiar situations lend an air of comfort
and security to our lives and depth to our relationships; too early an
adaptation makes for slavish compliance. Thus, non-adaptiveness can
strike a note for individualism in a mass society. On the more negative side, he can realize that his style may also be costly to him: he
may miss opportunities for more advantageous positions as he clings
to the routine and the familiar; he may find himself allowing his life
to become a treadmill of boring daily programming; he may find
himself out of touch with the world around him and with friends
who are more adventuresome.

We think this person can communicate to others what he knows
about himself and receive confirmation for this. We think he can
also communicate his need for others to play a stimulating and
encouraging role for him so that he can move ahead into the more
exciting part of life that he would otherwise miss. Although we
consider the Withdrawer a difficult marital partner because of his
need to control the interaction, we have seen some successful intimate
relationships and marriages among those who are Withdrawers but
who recognize and utilize the excitement and reward that understanding others can bring to them.

THE PERSISTER

In the Persister style cluster, the temperament trait that dominates
is persistence and this is augmented by the presence of slowness-to-
adapt, negative quality of mood, and sometimes a high level of
distractibility. On an interpersonal level, the Persisters see the external world as conspiring to silence and interrupt them. This
heightens their need to persist, which often adversely affects their
work and their intimate relationships. They are often left feeling
alone and unwanted.

The trait of persistence, of course, is an asset, and we are all in
need of some of this trait to keep us at jobs which do not reach rapid
closure. Without this temperament dimension, the tedious and exhaustive work which leads to creative "breakthroughs" would not
occur. People who are persistent work on their own creative work or

on "thing" tasks in a way that produces completion or conclusion. This is persistence put to work for accomplishing a specific goal, without being distracted into non-productive "spinning the wheels."

In its more troublesome manifestations, the Persister style cluster is most easily identified in the verbal dimension. It is observed as an endless, droning, volubility, using "um . . . and" as uninterruptible connectors between thoughts. We have also observed this in areas of motor activity such as jogging and swimming, where the actions become excessive and ritualized. Schoolwork and other intellectual or cognitive functions are carried out in exacting and perfectionistic ways. Furthermore, efforts to interrupt or forestall this overkill only serve to frighten or antagonize the Persister who sees it as an effort to keep him from the necessary efforts to achieve his ends.

We have found that the Persister has frequently enjoyed an active and successful childhood, and demonstrated productivity and "leadership" in many areas, capturing awards at school and camp. The Persister is given a sense of "closure" under these circumstances, marked by tests, promotions, awards. But in the more unstructured experiences of adulthood, persistence may become an end in itself that often leads to behavior that is ritualized, even compulsive. Lacking an internal awareness of "enoughness," the Persister needs some sense of having completed a process.

The quality of mood, as a rule, remains somewhat guarded and rarely enters the realm of joyful exuberance. Winning awards is not an occasion for feeling good, and compliments are shrugged off as if unimportant. Behavior seems directed toward denial and avoidance rather than toward experiencing pleasure. (It is possible that warding off the bad is a highly acceptable moral objective in our society. Positive enjoyment is a less socially structured experience and may represent a threat to persistent organization.)

Sometimes we see graduate students whose dissertations turn into volumes or who write and rewrite until they become convinced that they do not have the ability to write a dissertation and give up in despair.

Left to his own tasks, the Persister will at least proceed toward closure and a sense of having finished a task. But as usually happens, the natural temperament of the individual tends to be overused if one is not making use of interactive feedback as to how behavior is being received. It is in the use of persistence to resist and ward off others that interactive difficulties occur. Only if the Persister is able to accept the communication from others that they have "had enough" and is able to tolerate the pain of stopping when he does not feel like it, can he manage to "work with" his temperament.

The following vignettes of two Persisters will illustrate this style cluster as it is displayed in action.

Case of W.L.

This man is an accountant who is unmarried. When he begins to talk in group, he typically ranges far and wide, one thought or event stimulating another in a highly distractible way. He reviews the past week's evidence of how thorough and perfect he has tried to be in carrying out his work and how inconsiderately he has been treated by others, the very others for whom he is doggedly working. In spite of repeated exposures to routines of his office, he remains non-adaptive to the procedures and fearful that any work he does is not sufficiently finished.

He has had some short-term relationships with women, but is fearful that he will never find someone to marry. His relationship with his parents borders on the paranoid, and he constantly anticipates that parents and others will react to him negatively. His recent response to a suggestion that he join a beginners' bridge class, rather than follow his own inclination to learn the game by reading a book about it, was that he didn't want to because he would again hear himself berated for not knowing how to play well enough.

He first came for therapy as a graduate student frantically overwhelmed with the task of whether he could adapt to the procedures of his professors or maintain his own exquisite non-adaptive ways. It was obviously a matter of control and he was often furiously angry about having to go along with the classroom expectations. All of this had a strong paranoid flavor—it was a duel of sorts with the authorities who wanted to depreciate his intelligence by the forced intrusion of their own. He barely passed every course and failed at the C.P.A. examination the first time. Several excruciating years later, he retook the exams and passed after finally availing himself of the standard preparatory procedures he had resisted before.

His every life experience centered around the issues of "intrusive control." He was constantly engaged in warding off the intrusion of others. He was careful to run the water into his tub at the same "acceptable" hour so that he would not disturb or anger his neighbor. He constantly scanned all communications in order to apprehend any critical ones and begin defending himself. He lost several jobs because he did not know when he had done enough. Working as an adjudicator of claims, he was never sure he had covered all elements to be judged and therefore turned out decisions at a painfully slow rate. He was never able to successfully use any supervisory help or encouragement.

His interpersonal life was not only marked by this paranoid-like fear of critical intrusion, but he also had great difficulty in dealing with positive input. He longed for the warmth of intimacy but his need to be in control preempted that possibility.

In our work with W.L., we try to set limits to the amount of time he will be allowed to engage the group's attention to his problems and we try to set limits to the number of subjects he will be able to bring into the discussion. We also have worked with him to report only a positive event or interaction, thus attempting to work on emphasizing enjoyment even though his temperament enables him to emphasize discontent and worry much more frequently. We want to see him ask for and use information from another rather than fear this will demonstrate an inadequacy on his part.

Case of L.E.

This 30-year-old professional woman made use of her thoroughness and persistence to achieve top position in her very competitive graduating class. Her subsequent career, however, has not gone well and is marked by loss of jobs and inability to establish long-term relationships. Her fears of inadequacy are met by repeatedly setting tasks for herself towards which she must compulsively work for complete mastery. Any interruption, even a question about her work, is seen as threatening or interfering. As a teacher, she interpreted even questions from students as challenge to her—the student was seen as trying to show her up and dispute her grasp of the material. In her relationships she finds it hard to accept that others have any view of her except as regards her performance. Thus, she is sure no one will want to play tennis with her because she is not good enough. In fact, she plays so terribly hard with no evidence of enjoyment and with such obvious worry as to whether her stroke is adequate that it is really not something that others want to do with her. In our group we work, again, toward encouraging this woman to learn to use her relationships with others for some enjoyment. She is not without a certain sense of humor and her intelligence can lend itself to wit, as well as to proving her capability. The negative quality of mood seems to be hard to alter when her concentration is so heavily upon her need to persist in her tasks. We have also tried to get her to accept some limitations for herself, even to practice responding to a question with a frank, "I don't know," in hopes that she will discover that she will not then be forever discredited. We feel that the greatest communication need for Persisters is to be able to trust someone to tell them when they are overusing their persistence to the point that they are really preventing a sense of gratification.

On Being a Persister

As we have seen, this particular style cluster seems to be the one that is hard to relate to positively. In the Thomas/Chess study, the group of children who were called Difficult Children were the most likely of any of the style clusters to be referred for psychotherapy. In other words, their particular combination of traits seemed to be dissonant in their environment and they were consequently met with non-acceptance from others. In their continuing experience of being rejected, their feelings of anger, directed towards rejecting or interfering others, made them even more incompatible, while their own feelings that they were always being kept from pursuing what they were trying to do made them seemingly unable to get a sense of having adequately finished a task or an interest. Teachers in our acquaintance have reported their difficulty in working with children who persistently are out of step with the classroom routine and who insistently follow their own interests or, if pressured by the teacher, erupt with angry acting out.

Even so, the most "difficult" child of the Difficult Children in the Thomas/Chess study never developed any evidence of emotional problems. This child's parents found him not only acceptable but valued him for his non-adaptiveness, which was seen as independence, and his persistence, which was seen as laudable "determination." We can suppose that such a child could come to value these traits in himself and to make use of them in ways that were rewarding to him, thus avoiding the fear of failure and rejection that marks our adult Persisters. Apparently, what is needed is not the preparation for countering an assault on their activity by the use of their persistence to ward off others. Rather, we can see the person who recognizes this particular style cluster as needing: 1) relationships with others who can respect their need for persistence; 2) confirmation of their thoroughness; 3) communication that *asks* others to let them know when they are persisting too much; and, 4) comfort and reparative support when their way of behaving does not work.

9

The Adaptive Child Grows Up

When we discuss children who are "easy" to deal with, we seem generally to be thinking of them as being willing to go along with parents' expectations and society's demands. For example, an "easy" child would willingly go to school upon reaching what society has agreed is a "proper" age and would fit in with the school's routines, etc. This is to say, in effect, that the trait of adaptiveness is the major temperament dimension by which we decide if the child is "easy." The less resistance there is in the individual to accepting demands of others, the better the situation is for that other.

In parent-child interaction, the "parent" comes to represent the demands of the group or society in which the interaction takes place. Social psychologists have documented thoroughly that group expectations mold individuals' behavior. Resistance (being slow to adapt) to group pressures or expectations will result either in increased pressure on the individual or, if this fails, in ostracism of the individual from the group. Therefore, we see that the two style clusters in adults described in the previous chapter, the Withdrawal and the Persister, are made up of people who were slow to adapt or tended towards the non-adaptive end of the continuum. Our premise is that one's temperament is a "given" in the individual and that interfering with the behavioral manifestations of temperament creates a situation of dissonance for the individual. Thus, we see people who do have this temperament dimension of slow adaptiveness as often finding themselves outside the group or at the edge of the group, at least initially. How troublesome this is for the individual, or the group, depends upon how willing his environment is to accept his individuality.

Among those who were considered Easy Children in the Thomas/ Chess study, the other temperament traits, besides adaptiveness, that were a part of this categorization were regularity, approach, a positive quality of mood, and intensity that was mild or moderate, but not high. However, we have identified among adults with whom we have been working four other variations or combinations of styles which may have been present during childhood but were not easily identified as style clusters. These clusters all include, among other dimensions, adaptiveness of moderate to high level. We have given these four styles names which indicate the temperament trait that we consider the most important dimension for the style cluster we are trying to describe: *the Intenser, the Approacher, the Doer and the Adapter.*

It is easy to imagine that these style clusters could have been well accepted by many parents and the behavior manifested would have been reinforced by the approval of parents and others. The Intenser could have been experienced as a peppy, cute little child, the Approacher as the child who "never knew a stranger," the Doer as the successful child who could take care of himself, and the Adapter as happy and easy to get along with. Of course, it is also true that with other parents these same traits could have been disapproved or seen as undesirable, leading to parent-child dissonance.

People whom we identify as Intensers have often been parented by parents who found their intensity exhausting or socially unacceptable. As a result, these individuals have come to look upon their own intensity as something "too much" for others around them. The Approacher's parents may have found this trait upsetting to their accepted routines. The Doer could have run into difficulty with parents who were also Doers, so that a battle of wills over the child's activities could develop. Even the agreeable Adapter could have been looked on by certain parents as wishy-washy or lacking "spunk." The parent-child interaction in this case could have led the adaptive child to consider his natural temperament dimensions as unacceptable.

Changing expectations of behavior at various stages of life also impinge on the natural temperament in different ways. As a result, these temperament styles manifest themselves in adults in various ways.

As we get into adult stages of development and adult roles of parents and workers, the environment reacts in new ways to the temperament-based behavior. Needless to say, there are sex differences in these expectations, as well as developmental or age differences. The style of behavior that is admired in an adult male may not be approved for the adult female. The early studies of children do not show any direct evidence that temperament traits are sex related; therefore these differing adult role expectations (including the *style* of behavior expected) have had different results on adult men and women. We will try to deal with these variations in discussing these styles of behavior. For those adults whose temperament style appears to be dissonant with the expectations, internal signs of difficulty often develop and they appear for treatment with complaints of clinical distress. It is here that one meets symptoms of excessive and unmastered anxiety, depression, apathy, and the disturbing feelings of "going insane" or "losing one's mind."

THE INTENSER

The clinical picture of the Intenser is one which combines a high level of intensity with a low threshold of responsiveness, moderate to high persistence, and a quality of mood that varies. Adaptability is seen as at least middle level and will tend toward the quick-to-adapt end of the continuum.

This combination of traits is illustrated by persons whose communicative expressions are intense. Their body language is characterized by restless, spasmodic, sometimes jerky movements. There is a need for motion and activity, and the activity creates a dramatic effect. Every feeling is felt exquisitely and this shows on their faces, in their voices, in their words. Mirrored in their faces, their intensity causes eyes to widen or squint, foreheads knit, mouth and cheeks

screw up most painfully—as well as most delightfully when the mood
is good. Their voices fall and rise, words come out with a push at a
fast rate with high audibility, or else with slow, low, almost whis-
pered dramatics. Superlatives are the order of the day. Almost everything is said in its most exaggerated state. Heavily valent words—
"crazy," "monstrous," "nauseating"—are used. Hardly anything
happens in any ordinary context; everything is felt and expressed in
some special way.

Together with this, there is a low threshold of response, a tendency
to respond to stimuli with a quick rush of intensity. There may be
little restraint and the intense statement is out almost before one
knows it. The quality of mood varies because it is so charged by the
intensity. Once a mood is perceived, it is intensified to its highest or
lowest dimensions, which may give a "manic-depressive" effect. In the
effort to get recognition for their intensity which will bring them a
sense of closure, they may show a persistence and an escalation of
the intensity which will be perceived by those with lower intensity
as overreacting, unnecessary, even hysterical.

Intensers are exciting people to be around. Their heightened expressions lend a liveliness and charged air to all of their activities and
relationships. Such people will give the impression of tremendous
energy as they invest much feeling into almost every action. One of
our Intenser friends, now in his seventies, is having as intense experiences in his retirement as he did when he was a successful lawyer. We
were caught up in his telling of his newly developed love of oil painting and of his experiences of being a volunteer teacher's aid, teaching
creative writing to four-year-olds in a Montessori School. His voice
fairly quivered with enthusiasm and joy. And this had followed
immediately an emotional greeting which was nearly tearful in its
expression. We think that performers, particularly actors and ac-
tresses, possess this style of intensified expression, as do successful
sales people and, in fact, most people who are "people-movers." Can
one imagine a low intensity Billy Graham? The intense investment
coupled with the low threshold which makes them quickly aware of
the various reactions they arouse often allows them to have a quick
and heavy impact on those around them.

Intensers can also be tiring and irritating. As a result, many children who have been highly intense in their modes of expression have been given some very negative messages about this trait and closure has not been allowed to take place. With some, closure around positive feelings was allowed—it was alright to be exuberant and joyful—but negative feelings, sadness, or anger, were not acceptable. These people, who have not achieved closure around this "negative" style of behavior, are among our therapy patients.

We have found that women whom we regard as Intensers are much more numerous among our therapy clients than men, which leads us to speculate that perhaps the style cluster does not tend to be perceived the same way in men as in women. It occurs to us that men whom we might refer to as Intensers may be valued as "forceful" and this temperament may be very desirable in achieving positions of power and leadership. But, the very type of temperament which pays off in the world outside the home is largely devalued in wives and mothers whose approved societal role has been seen as supportive, somewhat self-effacing, and disinterested in personal achievement. In the past, women Intensers have sometimes been considered "bitchy" or even "castrating" and exasperated and mystified husbands often characterize them as "crazy" or "hysterical." It is not unusual for the husband to consider her a candidate for tranquilizers (as does the wife herself) or even hospitalization, since her temperament seems so ill-befitting "a proper wife."

Intensity also "ill fits" the disadvantaged in our society. Among those whom our societal arrangements continue to frustrate, we know there are many who will respond with intensity in the form of violent and antisocial behavior. Many people who are living at poverty levels in our cities experience the conditions of their lives as extremely frustrating. Lack of money, lack of opportunities, and lack of material assets that middle-class people take for granted are the daily reality for many people in our society. While some react to this frustration with passive resentment or even adapt to it and become somewhat indifferent or resigned, those whose temperamental style is intense will surely respond intensely to their situation and their frustration.

For the intense person who is constantly disadvantaged, violence could be understood as temperament-based behavior, just as, for the intense person whose life experience has provided him with positive goals and the means to pursue them, temperament is manifested in heightened drive and total investment.

Case of J.R.

This woman, in her late twenties, is unhappily married. Almost everything she does is marked by her intensity—she can be very vibrant and happy but also intensely sad and depressed. She is very sensitive to somatic feelings and expresses her awareness in exaggerated language: "I'm going to explode," "I feel spacy," "I feel weird," "I'm getting sick." In her relations to others, she exaggerates her effect and is constantly apologizing for "hurting" or "destroying" others.

She is the oldest daughter of a first generation family which came to this country from England. Her parents expected her behavior to be demure and unobtrusive and were aghast at her actions and at the unrestrained manner in which she expressed herself. Thoughts and feelings seemed to erupt and her reaction was a horrifying awareness of "Now I've done it again." Attempts to keep from arousing the anger and exasperation of her parents and teachers led her to hold back her intensity and focus her attention on this effort at repression, thus making her aware of intense body and thought processes.

The dissonance in this situation was the continual demand by her parents that she "keep her voice down" and "count to one hundred before you say something." In her marriage, she continues to find herself discounted by her husband who says she "overreacts," "won't listen to me," and "isn't like I expected my wife and the mother of our child to be."

We have worked with her in group sessions to show her that we recognize and accept her intense feelings without attempting to diminish them or extinguish them by soothing explanations. This recognition and acceptance bring her a sense of closure which is necessary for her. Without this transaction, the Intenser tends to step up his intensity. Now that J.R. is aware of her intense temperamental style, she is able to communicate to her husband her own self-knowledge of her temperament and her need for his acceptance of this. If he is unable or unwilling to respond in this needed way, we believe that she will either drive him away from the marriage with what will seem to him excessive overreactions, or she will leave him to seek a more accepting relationship. (It is apparent that knowledge of temperament and ability to communicate this knowledge to others will not automatically result in "saved marriages" or repaired relation-ships. Rather, knowing and communicating one's temperament and one's need for confirmation and acceptance may bring about a response that this cannot be done. If one spouse is unable, or unwilling, to accept the other's temperament, we think the deci-sion to continue the relationship or to break it off will need to take this knowledge into account.)

Case of G.P.

This woman sits very quietly, almost unmoving, in our ses-sions and speaks only slightly above a whisper. She is uncom-municative and must sometimes be prodded with several ques-tions before she responds. Sometimes flashes of animation or anger briefly appear, but somehow she quickly represses these and regains composure. Her face appears somewhat motionless though her eyes are very wide open and sometimes appear to be "pop-eyed," particularly as she struggles not to reveal her feel-ings. When attention is focused directly on her and she tries to explain her problems, she is unable to fight back tears, tears which seem to escape and give away her "cover" that everything is in perfect control. Although she and her husband have "never had an argument" in the eight years of marriage, she suddenly decided she wanted a divorce in order to be free to live her own life.

This woman was the younger sister of a child who died at a very early age and who, she always thought, had been "Daddy's favorite." Although her parents gave her everything she wanted, she always felt a poor substitute to them for the lost sister.

She is highly successful at her job and has worked very hard. She gets praise for her efficiency and her thoroughness. It is here that her intensity is employed in a way that pays off for her and brings her some sense of gratification. But in the area of feelings and emotional responses, she cannot get closure. It is a relief for her, from time to time, to indulge in behavior that seems bizarre by contrast to her usual tight control.

Though her husband becomes aware of her covert anger or sadness and directly asks her what's wrong, she refuses to reveal her complaint and maintains that everything is okay. Her reason seems to be that the feelings are petty and unimportant; thus, no one would really want to hear them. By clinging to a long list of unexpressed feelings, she finally has collected enough hurts to demand the right to be free of this relationship which in her eyes is insensitive to her needs.

We have tried to help her understand her temperament style and the extent to which she has worked *against* her natural style by inhibiting her expression and turning away from the possibility of gaining recognition and acceptance from her husband. We feel that as she learns to use her intensity to communicate her feelings and her own wants she will learn that others are not going to always consider them unimportant or unwelcome.

THE APPROACHER

This cluster is marked by a high approach, low activity, quick adaptiveness, fairly low threshold of response. Often this is accompanied by a tendency toward distractibility. These individuals respond strongly to what they think someone wants from them. Their initial contacts with others are from a position of readiness for stimulation and they seem to be presenting themselves to be found by the interpersonal object. Once found, they are largely focused on what the other person is asking of them and are strongly directed to go ahead and adapt to that.

A young woman in one of our groups reports that when she is on a new date or at a party with people not well known, she waits until she can pick up some cues as to what that person she is interacting with is feeling: "Is he shy? Then he needs me to be encouraging. Is he used to women falling all over him? Then I will be cool." Her behavior comes not from expression of her own desires, wishes or feelings, but from what she perceives to be the meaning of other people's behavior. Even though our client was *not* going along with the perceived expectation of the man who was used to women being highly attracted to him, she decided to act "cool" not because this expressed her real feelings, but because of the way he was acting. Her identity in the relationship requires a starting point of another person who strongly calls forth her responses.

When the person or situation approached is one that can provide a strong base for further growth and individuation of the Approacher, the interaction can be very valuable. This person can use his attachment to learn and to master areas which his own fairly low activity would never have gotten him into. In going along with the perceived expectation of an admired teacher, a competent boss, or a beloved friend or spouse, one finds that one has acquired new interests, new skills, and new ways of thinking what would otherwise be missed. One of our clients, whose own self-image was that she was fearful and somewhat incompetent, used her natural tendency to mold her behavior in terms of the wishes of her husband to become an excellent driver and an efficient and successful businesswoman.

Unfortunately, if the modeling person uses his power to manipulate or exploit the loyalty of the Approacher, then this person can end up feeling "used" and later rejected, with a helpless sense of "How did this happen to me?" As a society we are aware of this potential danger especially in situations when we almost position people to become victims. The teacher who is discovered to have "seduced" his students into actions or beliefs that are seen as harmful is a feared villain. Of recent date, there has been a great deal of accusation and counter-accusation as parents have tried to extricate their children from the "brainwashed" attachment to a group whose ideology they consider unacceptable, while that group itself thinks it has rescued the children from their parents' "brainwashing."

According to our theory, parents are misperceiving the situation if they believe that all people who are exposed to a new ideology will be so led astray. It is the temperament type known as Approacher that may, indeed, be so led. But other temperament types might respond by withdrawing, by persisting in their own interests and refusing to respond to others' pressure, by wanting to problem-solve in their own way, or in any number of variations of these themes.

It is true that the Approacher can become an almost unthinking victim in his or her loyalty and attachment to the idealized other, and can explain, interpret, and clarify for others the behavior of this model. Since they seek attachment to another, they are frightened if the attachment is not forthcoming and especially frightened if an attachment already formed seems in danger of dissolution. Once the attachment is made and utilized by the Approacher, then separation becomes next to impossible. We have heard complaints of being victimized or used for years by spouses or parents (and sometimes work situations or friends), but the individual seems unable to contemplate separation. Often, in response to the question as to why she is continuing a relationship so patently unrewarding for herself, a wife will reply, "But, I love him . . ." or "I would be lonely." When, or if, separation finally occurs, they feel completely abandoned and lost, maintaining a high degree of anger and depression around feelings of helplessness. Someone like this can apparently function all right as long as the original level of attachment continues. When it is lowered, there are, indeed, problems in proceeding by themselves.

When we deal clinically with Approachers, we try to emphasize to them the positive aspects of this temperamental tendency. Their low threshold of response and high level of approach to or acceptance of new people and situations make them ready for new experiences, and, if valued and recognized, can bring new zest and excitement to their life and the lives of others with whom they interact. Their quick adaptiveness allows them to get in touch with others. Often these people are artistic in either the graphic or literary sense where interpretation of character or situation is important. We try to get the Approachers to accept their style as their way of learning, mastering, and integrating their experiences. Even if they realize that it was the attachment to others that motivated them to achieve, still the achievement is theirs and cannot be lost. They have used this way to grow and become effective human beings. We think that they should maintain some good feelings about the value of their temperament position even in the face of exploitative experiences.

In terms of his reparative needs, we try to help the Approacher who feels used, abandoned, or threatened by loneliness after a needed separation to use others in his interpersonal network to help him evaluate the value of a new attachment or a new situation. With the interactive help of others and the ability to admit his own tendency to sometimes find himself enmeshed in relationships that do not work in his best interests, we think the Approacher can utilize his temperamental style productively and also protect himself from what may be harmful consequences.

Case of T.T.

This woman was divorced after a very erratic marriage to a man who was unstable financially and with whom she appeared to lose contact as he moved about the country. She has returned to her hometown where she has some relatives, but maintains her own apartment and holds a job as waitress. She is attractive physically and masks a fairly low quality of mood with a somewhat tentative and quizzical smile. She is not aware of any direct goals for her life but hates not being busy or occupied, so she takes up a variety of interests: tennis lessons, body fitness classes, etc. She appears to be looking for someone to attach herself to and if any suggestion is made she is quick to go along. She often ends up feeling used and taken advantage of and wonders how this "seems to happen" to her again and again. With the reluctance to separate, she found it difficult to take steps to divorce her husband even though the marriage had become completely empty. She waited until "he sent the papers for divorce," seemingly not recognizing that she herself could take direct action. In using the trust she has developed in her fellow group members to be really concerned for her best interests, she can accept her own "approach" temperament without allowing it to cause her frequently to act in gullible and naive ways. We have encouraged her to use others to talk over new situations and help her evaluate them in terms of being right for her. In this way, we believe she can keep from being victimized by her own readiness for new involvements.

Case of R.J.

This woman is also very prone to quick involvements and, like many Approachers, is very much afraid of loneliness. To others, the range of her interests and the wide variety of her friends seem astonishing. She is involved in intellectual university courses one day, a fashion show the next, a meditative out-of-body group experience the next. With a high quality of mood, she makes a delightful raconteur of her many experiences and appears to lead a full and rewarding life.

However, because she is always open and ready for whatever is available, her engagement with any particular interest must remain somewhat superficial or sporadic. She seems to have trouble making choices on the basis of her own needs and is thus constantly living her life for others. Even when these others are involved in exploiting her or in asking her to take actions which she does not enjoy, she finds it hard to separate from them since that would leave her without a direction. She feels that to separate from a relationship, even a bad one, is a "cop-out" and that she should be able to relate to everyone. She comes to therapy partly as an interest. We have the feeling that her involvement with us is part of her approach temperament—she has heard that what we do in our groups is interesting and she immediately sees it as something that she would like to experience. We, of course, have no objection to this way of coming in contact with our work. But we hope to use her involvement in this work to encourage her to recognize her temperament style and to understand that its value for her may be somewhat modified when she overuses this tendency to the point of dilettantism and to the point of being caught in situations and relationships that are painful or costly to her.

THE ADAPTER

The Adapter has a high quality of mood, high adaptiveness, low activity (especially in seeking out problems and solving them; in fact, he needs to be stimulated by the world around him), low intensity, distractibility and low persistence.

This person is characterized by being thought of as happily adaptable. Put in any social situation, he is capable of maintaining his high quality of mood and is experienced as empathic by others. Often these people are told, by relative strangers, about personal problems not otherwise easily shared. They seem happy and non-threatening to others. They are aware that since childhood their important role in the family has been to please others and often this makes for diverse adaptations. Pleasing one parent may mean doing well at school work, while pleasing the other parent may simply mean maintaining a happy, carefree, uncomplaining presentation of self, and pleasing siblings and friends may generally mean finding ways of avoiding direct disagreement.

What is striking about these people is the inner life. While all this pleasing adaptiveness is going on, they are often constructing and living in their own secret world. Their best (and more non-adaptive) thoughts are often savored only with themselves and there are moments of quick, tentative self-exposure hoping for an empathic encounter. There is a quick readiness for withdrawal in the face of any non-acceptance from another. Bringing their hidden "real" ideas out is often a tortuous process marked by frequent retreats and delays. This is heightened by an accompanying distractibility which, while a rich resource of ideational stimulation, can also be used for avoidance of the pain of exposure.

These people need empathic stimulation from the world around them to fully develop and expose their "mental" life. It is all too easy for them to deal away their high quality of mood to please and make others happy (or not unhappy) instead of using their mood as a personal motivational springboard toward creative insights. Often such empathic help is self-denied because the Adapter thinks that pursuing his own closure is decidedly selfish. Communicating their own needs is important in the temperamental economy of these people. If they do not pursue this communication, there is a high chance of depression with all the attendant radical responses, such as alcoholism or other addiction, obesity, gambling, suicide. Repair is often needed either to counter the effects of withdrawal or the effects of non-recognition or non-confirmation from others. Someone to share the hurt may be enough.

The Adapter does not seem to turn up in therapy groups as frequently as some of the other temperament style clusters. His ability to sense others' needs, relate to them empathically, and use his generally high quality of mood to support and encourage others makes him particularly valued and beloved. But sometimes the Adapter finds himself "ripped off" by demands of others and sometimes he finds himslef using all of his energy in the service of other people. Doctors are among those who sometimes have a hard time remembering that their own needs for recuperation cannot be ignored too long. It is not surprising to find doctors rating high among those who suffer addiction, alcoholism, and other symptoms of emotional overloads.

Case of B.P.

One of the men we have seen, who is an Adapter, has had a hard time working through his early married life. As a child, he was among the Easy Children: adaptive, good natured, physically active, and predictable. He was never a problem to others. Although he was very active physically and of high intelligence, his distractibility and low persistence resulted in schoolwork that was mediocre to poor. He seemed to find little excitement in pursuing academic subjects but was an excellent athlete and a real "team player." A popular boy with his peers, he often championed classmates who he felt were not being treated well by teachers, but with his respectful manners and naturally friendly approach was accepted even by these authorities. He married, before college graduation, a very active, achieving young woman, not without some misgivings as he sensed her as more dominant than himself.

Difficulties began when he began to move into the occupational world. With a fairly undistinguished academic record and a lack of specific skills (he had majored in history), he found job hunting a painful experience. Not used to pushing his own position, he felt himself tongue-tied in interviews. His work in sales, with its frequent rejections, was tortuous—each turn-down seemed a personal failure in relating to others. Meantime, his active wife was finding that success repaid her own hard work and was somewhat mystified by his lack of achievement. It has been difficult for him to survive these years with equanimity and this couple saw us with some despair over their worsening marital situation.

He had been spending several years adapting to the demands of a job that held out little in terms of personal satisfaction or satisfying opportunities for future achievement. Being empathic and sensitive to the needs of others, he had been aware of his wife's feelings of disappointment and of feeling trapped now in the mother role with two small children. He seemed not to have an opportunity to express his own ideas and his own needs. His usual sense of enjoyment and highly active physical and mental life were getting lost in a gathering depression. His wife began to complain that he drank too much beer in the evenings.

He has recognized the costs to him of overusing his adaptiveness and has used the encouragement of his wife and others to leave his job and start his own business. Given an opportunity to use his active mind for his own interests and goals, he is recovering his high quality of mood. As a small businessman, he is using his empathic skills to get in touch with the viewpoints of his customers. We see him as making good progress in learning that the temperamental tendency to adapt can sometimes result in the loss or diminution of his own needs and the expression of his own thoughts and ideas. We hope that he will continue to recognize his tendency to extend his adaptiveness in too many directions and will use this knowledge to establish priorities so that he will not devalue his own temperament style.

Case of L.T.

L. is a 23-year-old schoolteacher who, though not a patient, might be seen by some as straying into a life fraught with personal danger. The last four years of her life have been a period in which she has not only radically changed her religious affiliations but is now also considering an interracial marriage. None of this is being carried out with even the slightest hint of rebellious defiance. She is still the same happy-go-lucky, agreeable, involved person she has always been. In the light of her strongly adaptive history, her recent behavior has puzzled many who knew her. She seems fully aware of what she is doing and her only apparent discomfort is in not being able to convince some others of that. She is doing well in her career and shows no signs of her performance being affected in any deleterious way.

From birth on, L. was seen as a child who brought happiness into the family. She was a frolicsome companion of her siblings and, unbelievably, they even vied to take her places or play with her. She was agreeable to all parental suggestions and was well accepted at school by her peers and teachers. She went willingly to religious school and in public high school attained the adaptive peak of becoming a cheerleader.

The changes in her lifestyle in the last four years, though problems, seem to be positions to which she has devoted a good bit of thought. As with most Adapters, this change was germinating within her and was finally brought forth almost totally developed. Counter arguments at that stage were responded to by near acquiescence, but her ideas were never obliterated, merely shifted to a more private corner of her mind. At the present time she continues to demonstrate her strong desire to make everyone happy with her decisions, but is unshakable in their correctness for her.

THE DOER

This style cluster is marked by high level of activity, fairly high intensity, a variable quality of mood, and a lower adaptiveness than other style clusters in this group. A person with these dimensions is seen as gaining closure from active achievement. Given optimal environment, this particular temperament is rewarded highly in this society. We admire the Doer and feel proud of the person who can achieve and master his tasks. These people are generally our problem solvers and tend to respond to challenges with an orientation of "what is to be done." They will then get into the activity that will get it done. Their satisfaction and self-actualization come from the realization that their role is very important and from the evidence that this is recognized by others in terms of promotions and salary increases. Or, they are recognized even more simply by the fact that others turn to them when something must be done.

As mentioned previously, closure is often experienced via the route of active problem solving—the mental formation of the problem, its analysis and solution, and its completion. This leads to an elated feeling which, given full sway, may be verbalized as a kind of bragging. This special quality of closure comes from their own internal problem solving cognition and then action. Any interference with that personal sequence interferes with their sense of gratification and gives rise to discomfort leading to anger.

What becomes a problem for these people is their turning their drive for achieving toward handling other people's problems. If they see someone apparently floundering, they then see themselves as problem solving for that person. Usually, they have been successful as children in gaining reinforcement from parents for being a big help within the family. They "clearly" see the problems of others and their intensity pushes them forward into doing something to or for that other person. One of the double binds they set up for themselves concerns their desire to bring closure and gratification to the other. If their problem solving is rebuffed they may get angry, but then feel their anger as unacceptable because they may have caused some uncomfortable feelings in another which they then have to handle.

If most of the time their active temperament is turned toward handling problems of others (or others as problems), then they become habitually fixed into viewing significant others along the lines of "What's wrong?" and "What can I tell you or do about it?" This tendency to spend one's mastery on others has the eventual effect of depleting the self's sources of gratification and thus there is a tendency toward depression and, eventually, anger. Many of these people flip over into an unyielding helplessness and complainingness as if to say, "You will now have to take care of me and my problems as I have taken care of yours."

We also find that these people have a great concern with the possibility of failure. In fact, the two aspects, working toward success and avoiding failure, seem to be flip sides of the same coin. The high-active Doer who has learned in childhood that he is not good enough (not as good as an elder brother, not as good as his classmates) may turn his planning and active orientation to finding ways to avoid failure. This may come out in ingenious and elaborate alibis constructed in advance to avoid blame if things go wrong, or vocal complaints that he or she is overworked, fatigued, even ill, and so cannot be expected to succeed. Such a person may devote so much time to this avoidance activity that he performs less well than he is capable of doing.

Like the style cluster of Intenser, this particular temperament cluster is more valued in what we think of as the male role than in the female role. It is hard for the female Doer to stand supportively by and not problem solve or take care of all the problems of husband and children. When she does get into this behavior, she may run the risk of being labeled a "nag" as she tells her husband what to do about his business affairs and exactly how she wants him to perform around the house. When the Doer is a mother, she may "over-mother" her children to the point of interfering with their growth and development, performing their tasks much more efficiently than her learning child and all but taking over their homework and their social interactions. We view it as a healthy development, for this type of woman particularly, that old wife-mother role behavior is breaking down and that women can now manifest their high-active temperament in achieving in their own careers and interests with expectations that they will be valued in terms of salary and opportunities for growth on a more nearly equal standing with men. This woman can bring her own satisfaction in her achievement *into* a family rather than directing her temperament towards them and trying to get vicarious satisfaction from their achievements (with the covert thought that "behind every successful man stands a supportive wife," or "children owe everything to a good mother").

In our therapy situations we find more women than men in this category, but we surmise that this does not mean that more women than men are Doers. Women who are Doers are particularly torn right now with the old role that they, and their husbands, had learned was appropriate for adult women, and the current breakdown of these old role expectations. These are the women Doers who present themselves for therapy.

Case of S.R.

S.R. is a 42-year-old housewife who came for therapy because she was "at the end of her rope." She was in a state of anxious and ever deepening despair. This had come about as a result of an acute episode of sharp pain in her head—overwhelming and unyielding. Eventually the pain diminished but the patient thought she might have experienced a stroke and she could not rid herself of the fear that it would recur again and leave her a helpless invalid. A fairly self-reliant individual, she feared her fantasies of helplessness and becoming a lifelong drain on others. Her life history showed her to be a Doer who had done very well in college, pursuing a career in music. She had married early, had had four children, and had not continued her career direction.

She pursued her motherhood with the same dimension of high activity. Because her husband traveled much of the time, she was largely in charge of family functioning. She was an active, effective mother who thought a lot about her children and their needs and problems. Apparently she did not come to her husband for much help because "He traveled and why should I worry him." She did manage to play a musical instrument in volunteer situations, but usually in a supportive, "second chair" role. Her active self-image was always sustained by her constant ability to do her job well around the house and the satisfaction she received from that activity.

As the children grew, she found less consistent satisfaction because there was less need for her mothering activity. Before the "stroke," she had been thinking about what her future life was going to be. Was it all going to be behind the kitchen sink— was there nothing more for her? She had tentatively made up her mind she was going into musical education but was quite apprehensive about her present capabilities and not too anxious to face the challenge. When the "stroke" occurred, she was left with fearful possibilities she could not manage by herself any longer. Nevertheless, she kept her fears to herself and tried to battle her way through every day, but she was always left with the residual fears of further strokes and hopeless invalidism.

Only after her situation became obviously desperate did she seek some guidance.

In her initial interview, it was very easy to point out to her the importance for her of achieving. Her unyielding low quality of mood, anxiety, and fear of failure now necessitated a relationship with a concerned and supportive person. We were able to point out the traumatic nature of the "stroke" and that continued active behavior with support would most certainly help her. She was practically better after her first session and then decided to pursue her transitional development from motherhood to personhood again. This leap necessitated the supportive use of meaningful others to help overcome the anxiety of new, unfamiliar, challenging situations. As with many women, there seemed to be little support for a life other than motherhood. What seemed to help her the most was a firm grasp of her temperament structure. Prior to this, her life behavior had become too habitual, characterological. She had mastered motherhood and wifehood in a way that had become largely automatic, but she had no sense of her own effective self. Once this was raised to consciousness, she could then accept support and could be recognized for using her temperament for her own life.

Case of D.C.

This male Doer came to us for treatment when he had been laterally shifted in his company, an indication to him that he was being shelved, that he was "finished," that his contributions to important decisions in his company would no longer be sought. He had lived a very "successful" life, doing well in school and college, providing adequately if not lavishly for his family's needs, and climbing steadily up the corporate ladder. His high-active temperament had received the recognition of advancements and increased income and had provided him with a gratifying sense of closure. He took care of his wife and family, considering them to be dependents in every sense of the word, not only financially but in terms of looking to him for direction.

His unexpected shunting to another division, after a disagreement with a superior, was a sudden specter of failure, of inadequacy. Unused to being in the position of needing something from others, since he had always been the dependable one in his relationships, he felt very threatened and alone at this new development. Worrying about the fate of his poor dependents, his wife and children, if he continued his downward plunge and ended up out of work, out of funds, and fearing commitment to a mental hospital, he walked the floor alone at night in anguish.

It was not too difficult to identify for him his temperament cluster as Doer. He had gotten closure (gratification) from his ability to be productive and by this means had proven his worth. His role in his family of origin had been that of handling others' problems.

We have worked with D.C. toward communicating his fears of failure to others and accepting their reassurance of his value. He has been amazed to find that his wife responded gladly to his needs, saying that it was the first time she felt needed by him. As he recognizes his family as something other than dependent, and himself as more than head of household, he is discovering new dimensions in his family relationships. As he recovers his equanimity, he is again taking his active role in his new assignment and is working at recognizing his need both for confirmation of himself as a hard worker and for comfort and repair from others when fears of failure arise.

Part III

Temperament in Adult Interactions

10

The Fit of Temperament

in Interaction

In previous chapters we have been concentrating upon the identification of temperament. We first attempted to clarify the nine dimensions of temperament used in the New York Longitudinal Study as they appear to manifest themselves in adult behavior. Secondly, we described the style clusters that we have seen in adults, identifying sets of temperament dimensions that often go together. It is not our intention to have provided a list of style clusters which are either completely discriminatory or which are mutually exclusive. For example, when we speak of the Adapter, we are aware that his level of activity may also be a very important temperament trait. In fact, depending upon the particular circumstances in which this person is operating, we might think of him at one time as a Doer and at another time as an Adapter, as one or the other of these traits seems more important in understanding the dynamics of his behavior. The descriptions of adult temperament dimensions and adult style clusters are not diagnostic categories but are clinical or operational tools with which we can share information about temperament with one another, in clinical and counseling ways, and in our daily interpersonal interactions.

The case studies and examples which we have used, although meant to be helpful in the *identification* of individuals' temperaments, have shown the individual as "social" because it is in the social situation that behavior takes place. Interactive behavior as we see it is what takes place between individuals, each of whom has a temperament style upon which his particular behavior is built. An interaction which takes place between two individuals includes not only the consensual "meaning" which the parties to the interaction share but also the *way* in which each party to the interaction behaves. Neither of these is covert, and to grasp the meaning of the behavior one need not refer to "deeper" motivations or ancient "messages" from early childhood. The evidence is present in the transaction itself—each has made a "display" of his style in the behavior which has taken place between them as well as in the content of communication.

Since temperament is so overtly apparent, not only in the early spontaneous behavior of the infant but in the daily evidence of individual styles of behaving, it is curious that its importance in understanding interactive behavior has been so neglected. Of course, society itself serves to diminish the importance of individuality in interactions. In a large, complex, urbanized, industrialized, and bureaucratized society such as our own, there is little room for individualism. Most of our interactions mask individuality for they take place between people who see each other for limited reasons, for a short time, and who have only minimal expectations of one another. We shop at a supermarket and exchange a few words with a check-out girl. Our contact need not consider the individuality of either of us, nor of the owner or the store clerks.

Our interaction with the doctor, the dry cleaner, the hairdresser, may be equally limited, superficial and contractual. We each know what we can expect from the other in the transaction. Oftentimes, in a bureaucracy the rules are formally written and rigidly enforced. A supervisor may direct your work for the day. His or her supervisor may reserve the right to discuss your salary with you. In the Army, the officer will not have the sort of informal interaction which would be considered "fraternizing" with those in the enlisted ranks.

Society masks individual differences in other ways as well. Certain behavior is required, if not by law then by custom, in terms of the particular status which the individual occupies. One's socioeconomic class, age, and sex, for example, all carry the expectation of certain ways of behaving. Even more compelling are the "roles" which go with the status of husband and wife, parent and child, and "boss" and worker in an occupational setting. These rules of behaving often cover not only the content of behavior but the affect that should accompany it.

In a society that remains relatively static or in which changes come about fairly slowly, these contractual and role expectations remain stable and the society's requirements for compliance keep individual differences repressed. Institutions serve to reinforce these customary behaviors. The institution of The Family as commonly understood calls for certain role behavior and ways of carrying out these roles are prescribed—a "good wife" is submissive, self-effacing, a "devoted" mother to her children, and supporter-follower of her husband. A deviation from these expectations will mean the sanctity of The Family is being threatened. But in a period of rapid growth and change, the old contracts become obsolete and the old institutions continually shift. It is apparent that we are in such a period of change and that new opportunities for expressing individuality rather than repressing it are becoming open to us. One can almost sense it in the anguished cries of those who decry individualism in favor of outmoded institutions and who seek to keep or erect legal barriers to individual rights and choices.

Normative behavior thus shifts over time. The societal definitions of what is an acceptable range of behavior change under the pressure of the continuing tension that exists between individuals and the society in which they live. As individuals begin to test the outer limits of these ranges of behavior, then behavior that in an earlier period might have been considered abnormal can now be considered acceptable. In a society where there are wide differences in behavior in various subgroups within the society, then the overall pressure of the society in enforcing one common set of values and one standard of what is acceptable is weakened. The individual is free to adapt to a wide range of behaviors and this freedom is guaranteed by a shift of the force of law from emphasis on group norms to emphasis on individual rights. The very growth of society, which on the one hand takes away our individualism by making so many of our human contacts depersonalized and contractual, hands us back our individualism on the other hand by emphasizing our contractual "rights" to resist the "normative" pressures of the group. In such a society in motion, we seek ways of understanding our social behavior and of relating to each other. With the weakening of society's constraints on our close relationships, we face the confusions of normlessness and anomie unless some new ways to think of our relationships emerge. To think of relationships built upon the mutual recognition and acceptance of our basic individuality is the exciting possibility we have in our minds.

The variety of human behaviors we learn about in other societies are sometimes a source of wonder or amusement. It seems strange to learn that behavior which might be valued and strongly required in our society is unknown or perhaps strongly punished in another. In a society which is strongly communal, to harvest and consume what has been planted by someone else is accepted and sanctioned. It is *consonant* behavior in such a society. Such behavior in our society would be labeled criminal and would be, of course, dissonant. The behavior itself is labeled consonant or dissonant according to whether or not it is considered acceptable by the society which is, in a sense, interacting with the individual.

In America the quality of competitiveness is considered valuable and we socialize our children with competitive games to emphasize the approval we have for this trait. The child whose temperament may be manifested in high activity, high intensity, and adaptiveness will find that his temperament is consonant in this setting.

In a similar way, we believe that interpersonal relations can be consonant or dissonant. If the way of acting that an individual brings to the relationship is recognized, accepted, and valued by the "other," then the individual can feel himself confirmed and feel free to be himself in an open and spontaneous way. If his way of acting is rejected or ignored, then he will not feel recognized and confirmed and the experience of the relationship will be a dissonant one.

We use these terms to think of the wide varieties of individual temperament with which we interact with one another. If you, with your temperament, can recognize and accept my distractibility, then my behavior is consonant in our relationship. If you find my distractibility unacceptable and ask me to change it, repress it, or deny it, my distractibility is dissonant in our relationship. How much of my behavior as you find unacceptable is a measure of how much you have asked me to give up *being* myself. And though I may be willing and able to do this, there will be an accumulating cost to me in the loss of my individual self. It is this "cost" that we deal with in therapy groups. If my behavior is not acceptable to you, you will try to manipulate me into not expressing myself in the way you find unacceptable. If, for example, you find my intensity too overwhelming, you may manipulate me by scolding, punishing, or ignoring me when I display intensity. In order to hang on to our relationship, I will then have to suppress or displace my intensity so that you will not be confronted by it. However, if I am free to choose my relationships in terms of mutual reward of consonant interaction, I may decide that your inability or unwillingness to accept my way of being means that our relationship is too costly for me and should be terminated. Whether we are considering parent-child, marital, or any other reciprocal close relationship, the concept of consonance or dissonance is the crux of the interaction.

Consonant socialization (parent-child) involves a reciprocal giving and seeking recognition. This means that there is no manipulative intentionality, which is always seen as dissonance-producing activity. Once manipulative, non-recognitional behavior occurs, this leads to reciprocal manipulative counteractions—which clinically lead to greater and greater distance from closure and to more manipulation.

An illustrative case of consonance is the interaction of Daniel and his parents, Edith and Wally. Daniel, now a young adult, was born to a mother whom we identify as having an Intense style cluster, and a father whose style was that of an Adapter. Edith reacted strongly and quickly to many things around her. Physiologically, she was quite sensitive to heat and cold, always looking for the comfortable temperature. She was physically distressed by other elements in her environment such as noise (all music had to be played softly) and dull, dusty, messy rooms and furniture. Things she believed in, she believed intensely. She plunged into and apparently received a great deal of gratification from her religion and its ritualistic demands. Things were often black or white with her; people were either right or wrong; situations were fair or unfair. She felt these things keenly and easily expressed feelings.

Wally was rather inactive, preferring to think first before beginning action, and was often fearful that the action would be faulty and thus his thinking also faulty. He had a high threshold of response, and intensity was somewhat on the lower side. He was also quick to adapt and had a high global quality of mood. He was not a self-assertive person. Often content with feeding his good ideas to others, he hopefully awaited a confirmatory response. When his ideas were not well received, he rarely abandoned them; he kept them alive in his inner mental sanctum, working on them some more and waiting for another day for presentation. He found it rather easy, after awhile, to fit into almost any social situation, lapsing into a observer-participant position, going along, but thinking his private thoughts. Despite initial doubt and fears, he had a quickly emerging sense of optimism.

Daniel was a happy baby who seemed to enjoy himself at whatever he was doing. He breast fed with gusto and later ate his meals in much the same way. As a young boy, his sandwiches were almost all "Dagwoodian" creations gulped amid swigs from a milk carton. Food (that he enjoyed) was packed away at regular meals amidst sounds of satisfied slurping. Foods he did not like were forthrightly rejected. Daniel enjoyed activity but liked "taking it easy," withdrawing to play by himself for long periods of time, reading and watching television. He was seen as bright at his schoolwork but not particularly ambitious, nor inclined to doing anything extra. He was adept at many things but there was a limit to his investment: an excellent athlete but never a star; an excellent musician but unwilling to solo. He was always an easy child to get along with, rarely talked back, and agreed with most demands though he might not carry them out. He was not assertive and was always seen and experienced as pleasant to be with. We would consider his cluster as an Adapter.

Consonant interaction in his family unit was carried out in the following way. Edith was an intense mother. She reacted intensely to Daniel's crying for any reason and it was not easy for her to anticipate all the possible things that might happen and that he might have to handle. She was fearful concerning Daniel's well-being. This left Edith somewhat exhausted and vulnerable at the end of each day and needing to receive recognition and understanding from Wally. Often Edith would be "up" after a good day and "down" after a day of intense alarm. It was important for her to ask Wally to recognize and understand her feeling state. It was also important for Edith to look forward to getting back into activities in which she had invested before her intense involvement with motherhood. She needed support for that.

Daniel was a "good" baby for the most part and there was very little dissonance from either parent when he was a young infant. He was not terribly regular, but he was not demanding and when awake could coo and play for long periods of time by himself. Wally enjoyed Daniel's enjoyment of himself and found him always ready to engage in some playing and wrestling about. Daniel was skillful and took to new toys readily. There was some consternation on Edith's part because Daniel rejected being fully toilet trained. He continued to wet his bed every night well into his later childhood. Wally had the idea that this would probably end someday, but Edith became impatient and worried about it. She was able to get recognition for her worried feelings from Wally who was able to be supportive without having to "do something" about the situation. Daniel was aware of the social expectation and eventually saw its essential importance to himself. The problem ended when he wanted to stay overnight with friends. Daniel also experienced some problems around school, mostly around his passivity and distractibility. Teachers reported that he needed and responded to stimulation and without this would often lapse into a non-productive phase. Both Edith and Wally accepted the responsibility of stimulating Daniel around these social expectations of completing his schoolwork, but also accepted his distractibility as a necessary part of his thinking and creativity. As time went on, Daniel did somewhat better in meeting schedules. He was especially valued for his individual approach to thinking.

The recognitions that were reciprocally involved were of Edith's intensity, Wally's low level of activity and adaptability and Daniel's low activity and distractibility. Daniel's ready adaptability soothed many of Edith's worries. Recognition was given and asked for by the parents. Further consonant development would be for Daniel to recognize his need for stimulation and to ask for some structuring of activities which he might miss if left to his own inclinations.

Without the willingness to recognize and mutually support each other's temperaments, a scenario of dissonant interaction or socialization might produce the following. In the first phase of infant care, Edith might try to produce regularity, demanding that Daniel sleep and eat regularly so she could be assured everything was all right. Another dissonant reaction would be to demand that Wally do something, get the child straightened out! It might be even more dissonant to blame Wally for all of it. Wally might actually attempt to handle the entire problem and thereby feel increasingly inadequate.

Later there would be more demands for Daniel to stop his bedwetting: "Look what you're doing to your mother." "You do this only to annoy me." Again, Daniel could experience dissonance around his lower activity, distractibility, and generally lower intensity of involvement. The net effect of this might be to develop a general idea of ineptness and the impossibility of being understood. His school behavior could become more distractible and covert (inactive), with great needs for reassuring stimulation. Wally might very well have little to do with Edith and Daniel—Edith because she was always demanding that Wally do something to make her feel better or make Daniel do something; Daniel because Wally might feel inept as an active father who should be able to handle these problems.

CONSONANT AND DISSONANT PARENT-CHILD INTERACTION

Dissonance is seen as the outcome of non-recognitional, manipulative relationships. Therefore, any combination of clusters where there may be an element that can be construed as manipulative brings on dissonance.

Intensity in parents or child often leads to dissonance. It is difficult to live in the proximity of intensity without being stimulated by it toward some kind of influencing response. Intense adults often tell of remarkably similar responses of parents telling them, as children, that they were "too much"; "You're killing your mother," or your "father," or some other relative. Such children often embarrass parents who want to be adaptively accepted in their community. This intensity often becomes a burden that children struggle to bury; often they do, especially if they can turn their sensitivity toward concerns with others' feelings. This seems to happen to many women during their later adolescence prior to accepting the prescribed socially controlling role of wife and mother. This role assumption often is seen as a relief from the possible self-dissolution due to one's own intensity.

Children who are strong *withdrawers* also create difficult "fits." Their strong withdrawal, non-adaptive position obstructs parental attempts at closeness. This child is experienced as unhappy and rejecting—until such times as the inhibiting "anxiety" is mastered and an approach to interpersonal relationships can occur. Children such as these, who experience overwhelming discomfort in the face of others' approaches, want to assume some sort of control of the people in their environment. No one must make any change that creates interpersonal distress. There is also a concomitant fear of loss of the other and this too must be controlled. Parents who are looking for a confirmatory response to their own more positive quality of mood are often let down by this type of child. Seeing their child as unhappy, they often blame themselves or others, such as teachers or other children. It is difficult for them to accept the parental position of being understanding but firm in encouraging social relationships and new experiences. Even when the child obviously enjoys himself, he denies it and so the parent gets little gratifying confirmation or thanks.

Parents who are *Doers* can have a particularly difficult time with distractible children who are often seen as "lazy." This is especially true if the parental role itself is very important. "I can make it happen." "I must make it happen." "What will become of him or her if I don't make it happen?" This attitude leads to direct manipulation of the child, often from a discounting moral position. It is difficult for a Doer parent to let such a child develop responsibility for himself. The label of "laziness" is finally assumed which leads to a dissonant attempt to be active and efficient which can never be satisfied by the child.

Children or parents who are *Persisters* create difficult problems of fit. Such people cannot be rushed into shortcut completions. It is as if some process must be honored and any deflection from this produces anxiety. It is almost impossible for others not to attempt to hurry Persisters along and interference tends to be felt by the Persister as dissonant. Dissonance is only increased by efforts to manipulate. A Persister must know that he can feel free to pursue his own needs and activities and that his use of persistence is valued. In such an accepting relationship, he can recognize that he can curb his tendency to persist overlong.

In establishing consonant parent-child relationships, it is important to realize that both parties are seeking recognition of their individual ways of being themselves. Attempts to manipulate each other are usually counterproductive. The sense of gratifying primary relationships emerges from mutual confirmation and support.

CONSONANT AND DISSONANT MARITAL INTERACTION

Marital interaction is concerned with the fit of two adult temperaments. By the time we are adults, many other complicating factors have been introduced and the temperament that each displays to the other in marriage has been affected by the numerous vicissitudes of our own growth and development, as well as by the prevailing social conditions in which we live: the role expectations for husband and wife, the vocational directions we have chosen, the decisions we are making about becoming parents and about parenting children, to name a few.

Even so, we re-emphasize here our previous theme, that consonant marital interaction, like parent/child interaction, centers around reciprocal recognition and acceptance of temperament.

Unfortunately, many people about to marry view marriage in an idealized way as a state in which they will almost instinctively act and react toward satisfying the other's needs. In some cases this may mean providing a shield from loneliness; in other cases it may mean making the other "happy," changing or correcting bad habits, or giving the other a better outlook on life ("better," of course, to be defined in terms of the giver's own set of values!). Marriage may also be seen as providing the necessary role opportunity—to be husband or wife, and later father or mother, and to play out that role in some idealized satisfying way. Or marriage may be viewed as a way to escape from an unsatisfactory status or situation or as a quick opportunity for new relationships and new growth which will then bring gratifying change. In the glowing resolve to "do" for one's mate whatever is necessary to fulfill his or her needs, very few of us see marriage as a joint venture of reciprocal support for the development of each other. Some earlier recognition of the way in which the individual obtained gratification may now be suppressed in favor of playing the new role. Some dimensions of temperament may not seem appropriate in the new role or may not be welcomed or allowed by the new mate. In the effort to achieve a happy marriage, these dimensions may be muted and suppressed to the point that the individual is no longer conscious of them. Such "happy" marriages are quite vulnerable, for temperament has a way of emerging in unexpected ways at unexplained times. Suddenly, if "things" happen, a heretofore buried aspect of temperament is shaken loose and becomes activated. A marriage that has been falsely consonant on the basis of denied or unconscious temperament may be confronted with an awakening or opening up of consciousness of self again and dissonance unexpectedly enters.

Some examples from among our group members can serve to illustrate this. One couple maintained an outwardly felicitous marriage so that they were considered the most ideally suited couple around. Though she was very much an active Doer, the wife played a subordinate placating role of her dominating, controlling husband. He, though holding a menial job, took advantage of some inherited money to mingle with a much more affluent social group. He demanded her cooperation in playing the role of country club member, and dictated her choice of clothing and style of living. When she protested, he berated her for not appreciating what he was doing for the family. As their two children grew, the wife, restive with the leisurely suburban life, took advantage of a new opportunity to move into a well-paying job in a previously all-male work situation. While he welcomed the money she earned, her husband demanded that she account for every penny of her money and every minute of her time away from him. The husband's jealous demands now seemed to her to be complete non-acceptance of her new satisfaction in her own activity and she has decided that she cannot continue in the now open dissonance of their marriage.

Another couple had played consonant *roles* for many years of marriage. We identified the husband as a Withdrawer-Controller. He played his role as head of household: managing his household from the superior position of being sole provider, allowing expenditures, permitting activities that he felt comfortable with seeing his family involved in. The wife, B., was an *active* mother: managing children, contributing her share to familial and community expectations. Dissonance emerged when this housewife role became unfulfilling, and she began an enlargement of her capacity for activity and began to have less need to expend her energies meeting her husband's and her children's demands. Lacking her husband's recognition of the importance of her needs for self-gratification, B. began to see a separation impending and encouraged him to get help (therapy) for himself in order to live with her and accept her. In responding to his therapy, he finds himself rejecting his old role of head of household and wanting B.'s recognition and acceptance of his new freer lifestyle. Unfortunately, though both have changed their concept of their *roles* which had become no longer viable in this post-parental phase of their marriage, their temperaments remain. As a Withdrawer-Controller he now wanted to bring to her his new conception of his role as enjoying a new set of activities. She as an active Doer still feels unrecognized as an individual and feels that he is simply imposing a new set of controls. He is mystified that she is not satisfied with the new setup and sees her as utterly unreasonable and obtuse. She is also confused with her own feelings of dissatisfaction and wonders at her own unwillingness to simply play a new role with him, even though it is a role which does not hold out promise of her own gratification.

Dissonance or consonance in marriage can be viewed as *process* rather than a matter of compatibility of inherent temperament dimensions. At times, playing a role in a certain expected way may muffle or suppress an awareness of dissonance until or unless the role becomes "played out" or lacks fulfillment. Then the way of acting may seem stifling or lack meaning. In such cases, the partner may suddenly be confronted with new dissatisfactions and a fairly consonant-appearing marriage will become dissonant. If recognition and acceptance are not forthcoming, behavior may be misinterpreted as to its meaning and there will be an effort to get the other to re-establish the former "equilibrium." Again, if the social conditions permit little individuality and define role behavior very rigidly, the person who steps out of his role may be defined as "sick," and treatment will be desired to encourage "restoring" the individual to the societal definition of role.

Following are two scenarios for the same family, one with a consonant theme, the other showing how the same temperaments might reach a stage of dissonant interaction. The second scenario is a composite of several cases we have worked with. Its general theme of changing roles for women has become fairly common in our practice. We have here an example of the process of dissonance emerging out of an earlier consonance, pointing out our continuing need for recognition and acceptance throughout our lifelong movement through stages of growth and development.

A Consonant Case History

Mr. and Mrs. W.A. are a couple in their mid-30's with two pre-teen children. Mr. W.A. is a Withdrawer who is highly successful at selling insurance. As a Withdrawer, he has a keen mind concerning all possible exigencies and emergencies and is able to graphically impress his clients about their needs for insurance protection. He further offers the reassurance of assuming almost complete responsibility of handling and reviewing these insurance programs, so that bothersome details are kept to a minimum for his clients. He has an attractive, albeit sardonic, sense of humor which encourages relationships. His role is definitely that of the male protector, the father seeing that his children have every useful advantage, the husband keeping his wife happy and secure.

Mrs. W.A. is an Adapter with a high quality of mood. She can be counted on to keep things happy and humming. She has adapted well to middle-class expectations of motherhood, introducing her children to the conforming activities of the neighborhood, yet recognizing and accepting their individual responses. She gladly accepts the implied role desired by her husband and rarely pushes him to extend himself socially if he resists. He very much likes to stay with the familiar, and their life is tied up in their mutual relationships. She has found a good deal of stimulation in working as a volunteer for a preschool for autistic children where her cheerful adaptiveness is valued and rewarded. Another source of stimulation is involvement in sports where she works with the diligence and effort she used to put into her schoolwork. Happily, in these activities her husband is highly approving. She rarely takes a strongly venturesome step on her own and is happy that she generally pleases him.

There seems to be an open awareness of each other's temperament dimensions with some humorous gibes at each other's limitations, but obviously there is a strong acceptance. Surrounded by an ever increasing whirl of marital dissolutions, their marriage remains a kind of unique haven for distraught friends. Not only does the marriage seem consonant, but each of the partners seems personally consonant with himself.

A Dissonant Case History

A dissonant development of Mr. and Mrs. W.A. could occur if, for instance, Mrs. A. would become aware of some internal dissatisfaction with herself. This could be experienced as a nagging feeling of lack of self-fulfillment. Perhaps self-fulfillment is not the right word. If one has adapted strongly—pleasingly—there may well be a time of self-reflection concerned with one's own identity, perhaps a strong desire to experience the other possible essences of living. What we are suggesting is that the Adapters need new situations of adaptive stimulation, and if they are tied down in a situation that attempts to over-control their adaptive pursuits, this will eventually have an effect on them. Depression may be an eventual outcome and this may be marked by some attempts at compensatory self-gratification—eating, drinking, love affairs, etc. Adapters need "object" stimulation for adaptive purposes.

In such an event, we could envision the following "history." Mr. and Mrs. W.A. are experiencing difficulty in their marriage, with Mr. A. accusing Mrs. A. of no longer being primarily interested in him and the needs of their children. For the past several years, Mrs. A. has been increasingly interested in returning to school and this year finally decided to enroll full time as a degree-seeking student. Mr. A. has objected vehemently to this. He told her that he didn't mind one or two courses, but going full time was a complete rejection of the family, especially the children. Since her return to school, there have been numerous arguments about her "poor housekeeping" and the fact that she often goes out at night to be with people Mr. A. does not like or approve of.

Mr. A., a Withdrawer, says that for the first seven years of their marriage, Mrs. A. was a good wife who occasionally "goofed up" in some absentminded way, but who seemed to straighten out easily when corrected. She took "good care of the kids," but for the past couple of years she has become interested in politics and is now returning to school to study, "of all things," political science. In his attempt to get more attention and acquiescence from Mrs. A., Mr. A. engages in long, imploring arguments, and, at times, vindictively withholds necessary funds.

Mrs. A., an Adapter, says she has spent most of her married life going along with the demands of her husband and children. She looked forward to marriage and felt she was happy with her role. Mr. A. was somewhat difficult to live with—a bit exacting, but she did her best to be pleasing. A few years ago she found herself somewhat inexplicably unsatisfied with herself, a growing sense of her life seeming old and over. This feeling seemed to deepen and eventually led to her seeking counseling and relationships with other women "in the same boat." These new relationships were resisted strongly by Mr. A. who went so far as to "forbid" her going. Since her return to school, she has experienced her life as more alive in all dimensions, but wonders if she is doing the right thing.

Style Clusters Which Are Difficult Marital Combinations

In addition to the concept of consonance and dissonance as an emerging *process* in marital interaction, there are difficult "fits" of different temperament styles, which, of course, lead to dissonant marital interaction. In the earlier work with children, the Thomas and Chess group discovered that if a child had a combination of traits which they have called the Difficult Child, that child was predictably more likely to have behavioral problems needing psy-

chiatric intervention than a child with other temperament constellations. In our practice, we have discovered that certain combinations
of marriage partners seem to be predictably more likely to turn up
for marital counseling than others.

The most difficult combinations of marital partners we have
encountered seem to occur in relationships where one of the partners
is a Withdrawer. Withdrawers often develop a strong tendency toward controlling. Since they tend to be non-adaptive, they look with
suspicion on the adaptive propensities of their partners. The Withdrawer may view the world as hostile and dangerous and attempt to
keep spouses and other family members near and under control.
Often, before marriage, this "protective" attitude can be attractive
to those with other styles. Intensers, in fact, often feel they have the
capacity to bring some excitement to the Withdrawer's life and regard the relationship with a sense of mission. Although frequently
reinforced by the Withdrawer in the heightened excitement of
courtship, after marriage it is often a different matter. Intense expressions may now be viewed by the Withdrawer as "outbursts" or "irrational" and there are early attempts at controlling. The stimulating
relationships diminish as the interactions become centralized around
home and family situations. The Intense mate may try to carry out
the wishes of the Withdrawer, but this may eventually lead to depres-
sive reactions, and the Intenser may become clinically ill. Or, in attempting to restimulate his or her life, the Intenser may get into
behavior described by some clinicians as manic. The dissonance for
the Intenser will be a direct outcome of under-stimulation. In our
practice we have seen the combination of husband Withdrawer and
wife Intenser as a rule, but the reverse of this has also been noted
in several cases.

The Withdrawer makes a difficult fit also with Doers and Adapters.
The Doer attempts to relate to the Withdrawer by handling a lot
of situations which the Withdrawer might be uncomfortable about.
For example, if the Withdrawer expressed reluctance to go somewhere, the Doer mate would make accommodations to this by making
it unnecessary for him to go. She might go to the school meeting or
the community function alone or arrange their social life so that she

entertained a familiar few at home. This is part of the Doer's idea that she can relate by doing for others and becomes dissonant when she realizes that her own gratification is rarely achieved or taken into consideration. The Adapter, of course, wants to please, frequently has a global high quality of mood, and has the best chance perhaps for a consonant marriage with a Withdrawer. However, even the Doer and the Adapter learn that there is no end to their attempts to be helpful if the Withdrawer continues to rely on active control of his close interactions. He (or she) may remain strongly non-adaptive and demanding despite all the good intentions of the spouses.

A Case History of Marital Dissonance

Sometimes the dissonance in a marriage has built up over the years so that the cost of maintaining the marriage is too great even if the couple can be helped to see the way their two temperaments do not get any mutual recognition. Without recognition and acceptance by one's spouse, the feelings of hurt from being constantly misunderstood build up a huge backlog of defensive actions, usually retaliatory, and the dissonance reaches a breaking point. Such a dissonant relationship had resulted in physical violence in one middle-class, well educated couple.

Mr. W.E., who was a chief accountant in a large firm of accountants, was a very rational and cautious man. In his job his awareness of possible outcomes and his ability to "think ahead," to evaluate the outcome of certain procedures and decisions, were highly valued and sought. His Withdrawal type of temperament style, with its needs for resisting impetuous or not-well-thought-through changes, and his somewhat selective quality of mood were consonant with his job. He had become attracted to and married a vibrant, active woman. In her zest and high level of activity, she took over managing the family finances, the family social life, and the upbringing of their two children. In his uncomfortable feelings of being overwhelmed by this whirlwind of a woman, he struggled to maintain his sense of control by becoming dictatorial about certain actions of his wife. He found her cooking distasteful and demanded certain foods be avoided. He monitored the TV viewing so that programs he found unappealing were not viewed. She halfheartedly learned to handle these demands, actually going to a friend's house to see certain programs and not cooking some of her own favorite dishes. She busied herself with crafts and hobbies but even this met with his resentment.

Finally, his lack of appreciation and recognition of her activities and his inability to appreciate her need for such confirmation of her as a person led her to decide to go to work outside the home. He was outraged at this and considered that she had failed him as a wife and that her insistence on working outside the home was the cause of the behavior problems of the children, which had emerged in this dissonant family situation. His need to regain control over his family led to increasingly bitter confrontations, sometimes ending in physical attacks on his wife.

We worked with each of them in different groups, helping them to recognize their own temperament dimensions and how their separate needs for recognition have not been met in their marital interaction. They responded with surprise at this identification of themselves and recognized their failure to accept the temperament of the other. The wounds of past encounters made it very difficult for them to see any future in developing a more consonant relationship. However, each began to see that the success of the future intimate relationship would depend upon a willingness to know their own needs and also to "allow" and confirm the temperament-based needs of the partner. The husband is beginning to recognize that his wife's satisfaction in lots of activity is due to her own highly active temperament and is not instigated to upset him or challenge his tight controls. For her part, his wife has begun to recognize that her tendency to respond to his controlling demands by high-handed circumventing of his wishes behind his back does nothing to reassure him in his fears of loss of control.

We have seen several people with strong Withdrawal temperaments demonstrate their determination to control others with whom they interact. We witness their almost frantic escalation of demands on the other—they seem to think that to keep the relationship they must win some sort of battle of wills. This often takes a form of vindictive manipulation and, surprisingly, physical coercion. It is "surprising" to find this physical coercion on the part of a Withdrawer husband because he often appears in the clinical setting to be rather like a timid child. There is enough ensuing violence in such interactions that we have begun to hypothesize such a temperamentally dissonant relationship in stories of child and spouse abuse.

Counseling Dissonant Marriages

When we work with couples who have marriages which have become dissonant because they are difficult fits, we cannot be sanguine about helping them achieve consonance in their marriage. We believe that temperaments will remain fairly consistent and that the Withdrawer will not become an outgoing carefree spouse whatever the mode of therapy. Nor will the Intenser learn to live with little or no stimulation, nor the optimistic Doer learn to be cautious and content with inactivity. When we see couples in marital counseling, they have often already passed the point of no retreat from complete dissolution. About the best thing we can do is help them recognize temperaments and the way their interactions in marriage have reflected these temperaments. Often they are able then to accept the separation without the sense of angry blame and can arrange their affairs and the decisions about their minor children more responsibly. Hopefully, in future intimate relations, they will be able to use this knowledge about themselves. We believe that recognition of temperament dimensions, in self and in one's prospective mate, before marriage and *before* hurtful recriminations due to non-recognition have accumulated, holds out the promise of more gratifying relationships in marriage. If parent-child interactions can be helped to prevent dissonant behavior in the early years, we are hopeful that intimate adult relations based on such recognition will prove to be a way to prevent dissonant marriages.

OCCUPATIONAL INTERACTION

It is not only in parent-child interactions and in marital interaction that consonance and dissonance of temperament play an important part. For most of us a large part of our interactive life occurs in a work situation. Many factors are involved in job satisfaction, of both a social and a personal nature. One of the more neglected aspects is the relationship of the job to the individual temperament of the person performing the job.

Difficult occupational fits generally occur because temperament dimensions are not recognized. When interactive difficulties are apparent on the job, it is much more usual to look for the reason in some sort of "ineffective" communication or in some lack of motivation or inadequacy on the part of the worker. If, for example, intramural reorganization is necessary and people are shifted to different offices, different supervisors, or different time shifts, we can generally observe that some people become very resistant and show this resistance in a variety of obstructing ways. A supervisor might think of this as some sort of "troublemaking," even insubordination. The resulting dissonance might have been avoided if the worker could have been recognized as a Withdrawer for whom change is always experienced as uncomfortable. A longer lead-in time or simply the assurance that his discomfort was recognized would have allowed time for him to get used to the new arrangements. Withdrawers are not inadequate workers; when they are allowed to proceed at a more comfortable pace into new situations, they frequently outperform their more quick-to-adapt colleagues.

It is also true that some temperaments seem dissonant with certain types of jobs. Doers do not do well at jobs of restrictive movement. Routine work, with no problem-solving opportunities, is draining and exhausting. They need new challenges and shifts. Withdrawers, on the other hand, like to settle into the familiar and seem most satisfied when they can experience some control over the day-to-day circumstances of their job.

We have, in our clinical practice, seen many people whose current experience of depression or self-depreciation is directly related to their job experience. As they are unable to obtain a sense of closure or gratification in this important area of their lives, the sense of inadequacy and unhappiness begins to spread to other interpersonal situations and may lead to overwhelming despondency, even suicide. The following case histories illustrate the crippling effects of dissonant experiences in the occupational sphere.

Case of S.I.

A 30-year-old married man came for therapy, drinking excessively, his life on the verge of disaster. The drinking had begun about six months before and was basically used to cope with severe losses of self-confidence, a quality he had proudly presented to others up to then. Our observations showed this young man to be an Adapter who had dedicated himself to pleasing his parents and who took on a rather high degree of expectation of self-sufficiency. "I should be able to make myself happy and confident." "I should be able to handle the stresses of my job alone." "I should always look confident, even if I don't feel it." "I should be concerned about other people's feelings and help them."

As an Adapter he had done well on his job, which was media sales. Although he often "mumbled" to avoid unpleasant confrontations, he apparently was personally accepted and appreciated. This showed in his sales record where he led all the other salesmen. He was eventually given a promotion covering a different type of market and a much larger geographical area. His adaptiveness made him quickly aware that sales in his new market had not been flexible enough in price to be competitive, but he feared displeasing his bosses with this information. When he finally presented his plan for more leeway in setting prices for sales, based on his understanding of the real situation, it was flatly turned down. He was given no recognition of his adaptive knowledge of the sales situation and was told to stick to rigid pricing, where he felt he could not succeed and would be acting against his judgment of the situation.

His response to this impasse was a severe loss of self-confidence. His company apparently could not understand the situation or his shaken response to it. He began to bolster himself with a few drinks. All of this created more awareness of dissonance which only led to more drinking to blot out the whole problem. In this case, the dissonance became apparent when there was no recognition of this man's individuality in carrying out his job. His particular way of evaluating the market, by using his adaptive temperament to get in touch with the situation, was not confirmed and he was left feeling that he was inadequate for the job. It is quite possible that his assessment was one that his bosses were unable to operate with, which made its rejection necessary. But if they valued this employee (and they had been satisfied with his past performance enough to promote him to this new spot), they could have recognized his understanding of the situation as valuable information and then made the decision to accept or reject this information.

Case of M.M.

M.M. was an engineer in his early 40s who had experienced most interpersonal relationships as fearful encounters. His temperament identity was that of the *Withdrawer* style cluster with its slow-to-adapt component. He feared and loathed his father's "superiority"; though he generally felt inferior to others, paradoxically he thought he was often smarter than others. This combination often led to a kind of challenging questioning on his part that disturbed others and made them retaliate. His career development seemed uneven. At the time of entering our group, he was anxiously stymied on formulating his Master's thesis and was quite dissatisfied with his job. He was not happy with his job stature, nor was he happy about the nature of his work or the people he worked with. Much of his dissatisfaction had to do with a sense of his not being recognized. He had what he thought were good ideas, often better than his colleagues', but his tendency toward withdrawal made it almost impossible for him to present these ideas. As a result, he would end up with a sense of righteous superiority, somewhat alienated from his co-workers and certain he was going to be fired. We encouraged him to seek closure by asking for encouraging support from some of his colleagues, but he experienced that as "too threatening." His behavior at work could be seen as dissonant, but the basic source of it was within himself. Unless he can learn to recognize his needs for support, this dissonance, and the consequent difficulties, will be carried to the next and the next job.

Case of J.B.

Another example of occupational dissonance concerns J.B., a young unmarried man who experienced dissonance on his first job after graduating from college. J. was a media reporter who had apparently enjoyed working as a student manager for his university radio station, but found that a job in the private media industry was another thing. He was an Adapter who wanted very much to please and needed to get some confirmatory feedback. The organization he worked for was very demanding and essentially non-supportive. It was prone to express itself with worried outbursts, and never showed any special sensitivity to the help J. needed nor to what he was accomplishing. From time to time, J. would clearly state his need to have his thinking confirmed and recognized, but this seemed to be one of those places where you were expected to do your job and expect nothing in return. He finally began through sheer experience to have a sense of being able to do his job and began to regain his equilibrium and good quality of mood. His work became more productive but still recognition was not forth-coming.

After a year of trying to please and getting no confirmatory recognition from his bosses, he finally asked for a raise in his obviously insufficient wages. When the usual demurral occurred, he finally decided to quit and seek a more rewarding work situation. The dissonance was around the complete inability of the organization to recognize J.'s individuality by expecting him to function as not needing confirmation. It is interesting to note that turnover in this organization is extremely high.

When temperament styles are recognized and supported, job satisfaction can be high. This happy situation can occur if there is a realization that work does not always turn out to be perfectly executed and that even in the most compatible work situations problems will arise. If temperament is recognized and the individual is aware of his needs for gratification through the confirmation and support of others, an occupational experience can add an important dimension to ego strength.

Case of E.L.

An example of occupational consonance is E.L., a secretary. She is an Intenser who invests strongly in what she does. Doing not only brings with it a sense of completion, but an exhilaration. At the same time, there is often an accompanying sense of apprehension which at one time may have been used to avoid further investment. Often in the past she had become over-involved with "handling" uncomfortable feelings of others, but now she is determined to pursue her excitement toward more personal goals of fulfillment. Her employer is aware of her intensity and attempts to give her projects which can be vehicles for her intense investment. Despite her hints of inner fear, she seeks and uses encouragement to sustain her course until she experiences closure and gratification. When she is depressed or discouraged, this is accepted with the expectation that more positive intensity will again enter the picture.

Case of R.B.

Another example of occupational consonance is R.B., a school teacher in her late 50s. She is a Doer who unfortunately has had to "handle" a number of personal tragedies. She has always sustained the dimension of effective action and solved problems which might have seemed overwhelming to others. She might very well have been successful at a number of "men's" jobs, but the career she was pointed toward was the acceptable "woman's" one of elementary teacher. She has always seen her job as a challenge and has done well. The education of a child is a source of particular gratification to her; she is positively encouraging and gently persistent. She communicates verbally her investment in the children, both her joy at their successes and her concern with their problems. She gets a good bit of recognition from her principal and other supervisors. Non-successes are experienced as dissonant, but she is generally able to get repair from helpful intimates around her and charge back into action again.

CONSONANCE AND DISSONANCE IN CHANGING ROLES FOR WOMEN

Because of the widened interest in the occupational world on the part of middle-class women, we have seen some interesting examples of what happens when temperament is viewed differently according to the role that is being played. In identifying what was considered feminine behavior, both sexes in the past have agreed that it was unfeminine to be competitive, forceful, loud, or demanding. Thus, a woman who was highly active or quite intense could feel herself under some criticism for such dimensions; yet the occupational world values the same traits and rewards them. As women move from the sphere of home and children to the occupational sphere, their own thoughts about *how* they are being themselves undergo some changes.

Recently we interviewed two women in their mid-30s pursuing active careers, after putting in some years as wives and mothers. They had both been participants in a workshop where we had explained and worked on temperament identity. As they worked in the group, their clusters became easily apparent both to us and other inexperience members of the workshop. What they told us is that they definitely did not recognize themselves the way others saw them. One was a Doer and the other an Intenser, but because of a combination of family and cultural conditioning, the Doer diminished her essential doing competence because she felt that to be uncomfortably competitive (and women must not compete). The Intenser denied this dimension because it implied a lack of control and she had taught herself the special importance of emotional control for a woman—whose ultimate control was in marriage.

These two women are striking examples of self-non-recognition. They may function quite satisfactorily at their occupations and yet experience a certain sense of dissonance in attempting to sustain the denial of temperament dimensions. Not being competitive may stand very much in the way of closure so that one might be left with a nagging sense of unimportance. Not being intense may lead to a depleting, unstimulating life of borderline depression, tiredness, apathy. In a sense, self-recognition is not wanted by these women because each of them may be heavily into manipulation of close relationships through their denials. To become aware of the deficiency of self-recognition could lead to cessation of the self-denial and clearer expectations of response from close ones. The Doer might now wish to assert her temperament and ask for recognition from a spouse who has been manipulated into thinking of her as not finding her career really stimulating and important to her. The Intenser might feel that to continue to live with someone who could not appreciate her feelings would no longer be possible for her. Yet their careers will remain ungratifying and their achievement only mediocre if each continues to hold back or muffle these important dimensions of their temperaments.

11

Communication for Recognition and Repair

In earlier chapters we have talked about the recognition and acceptance of one's own temperament style and of the necessity of recognizing and accepting the temperament style of others with whom we are in interaction. We have also noted that when we are interacting with one another we discover there is a consonant or a dissonant "fit" which depends partly on our ability to identify and communicate our own style and partly on the willingness and the ability of partners in an interaction to recognize and allow the temperament style of each other. Our interest in the interactive aspects of temperament styles arises not only from the fact that our lives are social and thus we construct our behavior in respect to others, but also from our conviction that we cannot really be our "self" without the interactive response of others. We cannot know who we are except by experiencing that we are knowable to others and that they do recognize us. Our sense of self (autonomy) depends, then, on our ability to communicate or display ourselves and to have this confirmed by others. We refer to this sense of confirmation of our way of being ourselves as closure.

At first glance, this dependency upon others seems to demolish our intended emphasis on individuality and autonomy. But we have been forced to believe that real autonomy exists only in interaction with others. We are convinced of the primacy of relationships in our lives and we have seen numerous instances where painful isolation has resulted from the lack of supportive recognition and acceptance from others. Many people strive for an unrewarding independence and miss the gratification of interdependence, where people assist each other toward autonomy. When individuals clearly communicate their temperament style to others for closure, this has often led not only to the development of deeper intimacy but also to a greater sense of identity and satisfaction.

The shift of psychological thinking toward the ego disorders (character disorders, borderline disorders, narcissistic neuroses, etc.) has been accompanied by an intensification of the study of "self." Starting from the pathological, early studies were concerned with the mechanisms of ego defense. This orientation of ego as defense has become increasingly unacceptable. Much as Freud reacted to his early findings of incest with the conviction that there just could not be that much incest, the ego psychologists could not accept that the dominant ego function was defense. There was a growing acknowledgment that ego functions must also be involved with growth and development and with the uses of intelligence. Erik Erikson and others have emphasized the connection of the sense of ego identity with phases of growth, especially as conditioned by socialization. This view sees identity as substantially mediated by growth and by role expectations, modified by inner drives and modes of reaction. In other theoretical approaches, identity was more tied to social role performance, i.e., the way in which we were performing an identifiable role, a role which we learned or were manipulated into performing. We were born to be socially identified and role defined, and if we did not become what we were expected to be then we were likely to be seen as deviant. In such a view, deviance also comes to be socially defined and "character disorder" is seen as behavior that is outside the range of acceptable role performance. It was taken for granted that children were socialized, manipulated, and handled by parents in good or bad ways, and that this socialization positioned the children in good or bad directions. If only a child were fortunate enough to have enjoyed unerring parenting, unacceptable behavior would not occur and a child, any child, could achieve any desired identity.

Accepting the findings of the New York Longitudinal Study, we would say that these ego identity formulations do not recognize the actuality of self as it exists and appears to others, an actuality which includes "given" temperament dimensions. In this view, one is not identified through role assumptions but through the temperament dimensions of response that often occur grouped into clusters. These clusters are our style. We *are* our style. Our behavior (which, of course, includes individual talents and abilities as well as cognitive and attitudinal input from our environment) is characterized by a display of our given individuality, a recognizable "how" we are being ourselves. A display is a manifestation to others and is necessarily tied to a response of recognition.

Communicating one's temperament to others for confirming recognition involves, first of all, the capacity to see and know one's style. The general tendency of ego organization towards habitualness makes for less and less consciousness of self. Communication of one's temperament involves recapturing the essential self-consciousness we have dimmed. This is not an easy thing to do. Our first objective is to reestablish consciousness of the dimensions of an individual's style.

A great majority of our patients present themselves suffering from a failure of self-recognition and from the effects of living lives of dissonance. Our first task is often to interact with them in a way in which they can begin to establish primary self-recognition. Using the New York Longitudinal Study's nine dimensions and our extrapolations to adult style clusters, we help them to a conscious recognition of their inherent individual temperament style. We want them to know we are not going to "change" them, but simply to help them to identify themselves through their cluster of temperament dimensions.

There are several initial reactions. A reaction we often get is dumbfounded disappointment. "You mean to tell me that I can't change?" "Are you telling me that I am doomed to be the inadequate person that I am?" These are people who have been in profound states of dissonance within themselves, excoriating themselves, and seeing therapy as a last resort for their redemption. Another group reacts in a grateful way. "You mean I'm not really crazy?" "It's alright for me to be me?" These people generally respond with cautious acceptance of the concept of identifiable temperament, often backed up, if they are parents, by their own observations of early-noticed differences in their own children. Still another group reacts with disappointment to the "no change" policy, for they have come to therapy primarily because they found others difficult to relate to, and they are seeking ways to actually manipulate and change others (spouses, children, etc.). We have to repeat over and over again that not only are we not out to be agents for changing them, but that they cannot be agents for changing others.

But patients who have gone beyond the initial fears of "not changing" are by no means finished with their resistances. There may be not only general resistance to self-identification but also simply an inability to conceptualize oneself as acting in a way that displays one's temperament. We generally work on the self-identification process in groups where there can be feedback of information from various people in the group. Dimensions of temperament that seem clear-cut to the group members sometimes seem surprising to the individual himself. His temperament has often been unrecognized by him, and he feels somehow that he has been suddenly unmasked.

We recognize that self-identification usually has a tentative, fragile existence until it is confirmed by recognition from others. It is as if one is asserting one's identity in some forbidden, selfish, isolating way and there is a tendency not to want to take credit for being one's self. We are struck by a strong tendency to deny one's self-ness, as if this might bring on some dangerous separation or rejection. Previous relations have built upon early interaction with parents which produced a consensual validation of self. Identification has been further tied to assumed roles. It is as if the person realizes for the first time the actual self-identified dimensions of her individuality as separated from an identity imposed by others. Though she recognizes the validity of this and wants to claim it, she is also struck with the vulnerability of needing to communicate this identity and needing the actual confirmation of recognition.

COMMUNICATION FOR RECOGNITION BY OTHERS

Even after an individual has been able to recognize his own style, with the help of feedback from others, his consciousness of his temperament style is not easy to communicate to others. There is a feeling that such directness is unseemly, that one should hope to be recognized by others intuitively. It is a residual romantic notion that someone will be found somewhere who will look into our eyes, recognize us, and love us, "though not a word is spoken." The fact that this does not seem to happen, outside of grade B movies and pulp magazine stories, does not seem to squash the yearning nor dispel the secret conviction that this could be our lucky destiny. Failing this, it is conceded that our more likely fate is to try to adequately fulfill the role we have taken on, or have been manipulated into accepting, and to thus "deserve" the recognition of having performed well enough. There is no dearth of advice on how to be an "effective parent," a "total woman," a "winner" instead of a "loser." The idea seems to be that one can be whatever one wants to be—just follow the five simple rules! But to think that one can be recognized for the way in which one goes about living one's life seems too radical an idea for many. And to state one's temperament style and ask for confirmation seem too much like programming others. We often hear, "But if I have to ask someone to recognize me, it's not worth it." "But she should know that about me without being told." So we often settle for hiding our disappointment in others' lack of understanding, or we try harder to manipulate the response that we refuse to ask for.

Finally, in addition to the resistance that comes from the feeling of vulnerability in disclosing the "real" self instead of the self that we have accepted through socialization and role definition (resulting in a reluctance to communicate directly instead of trying to promote indirectly), there is often another layer of resistance to communication, the "weakness" of needing others. Our conviction that one cannot become or be a fully autonomous individual without the recognition and confirmation of others seems a contradiction to many of our patients. In our society, particularly, there is a high value placed on self-confidence, self-esteem, and the self-made person. Independence is held up as a strength, and the "self-controlled" individual is the paradigm of the whole, integrated, emotionally stable person, the very goal for which we are taught to strive. We have heard again and again from our patients, "I shouldn't need someone else. I shouldn't be dependent." To admit need for someone else is, in the minds of many of us, to admit to weakness or immaturity. So when we stress the need to communicate to others who we are so that others can confirm our knowledge of ourselves, we run into these stone walls of resistance.

The task is to acknowledge our own self-identity *and* the identity of others. We think of this as a higher level of consciousness. It exists most effectively in relationships of confirmatory recognition, acceptance and support, and surely must dominate the substance of intimate relations. Sometimes simple recognition is sufficient (the Intenser simply wants someone to know that he feels very strongly). Sometimes acceptance is needed, the sense that, "Even if I do not share your style of behaving, I do accept it and value it as your style." Sometimes, claiming our identity and acting on it will need the support of others. There is often an affective component accompanying behavior: the Doer experiences some fears about his competency; the Withdrawer experiences anxiety in new situations; the Intenser fears that his feelings will be overwhelming. What is needed is the support of someone else so that the individual can proceed toward closure in spite of these affects.

Successful interactions, then, for each of us depend upon this communication of ourselves for recognition and confirmation from others throughout our lives. If we have been recognized and accepted as children, we can be seen as achieving a happy self-identity upon which to build successful adult relationships. But, if this recognition is denied us in an adult interaction, we cannot feel that the relationship is successful or that we are happy in it. Many marriages falter simply because people are not emotionally gratified in the marital interaction. From an older institutionalized position of marriage as a lifelong contract, we now see a new position which seems to be, "If you're not 'happy' in this marriage, why should you stay in the marriage?" While strong moral sanctions or economic realities may keep people in marriages that "successfully" last a lifetime, such "successful" marriages do not always provide the emotional well-being that can grow out of a more soundly based relationship. Thus, while many decry the high rate of divorce in our society (and we are certainly aware of the heavy toll of "broken" families and the real suffering of minor children when their security is breached) , we feel that helping people to communicate their needs for recognition of themselves is a more realistic way to better relations in marriage than simply strengthening the institutional supports of marriage and family.

A Case of Non-recognition

One of our group members was an active middle-aged woman whom we identified as an Adapter with strong intensity and a positive quality of mood. Unable to get a sense of gratification or fulfillment in her long-time marriage, S. struggled with a sense of guilt over her decision to leave this marriage. She reported a rather joyous childhood in a large family in which she was recognized for her happy disposition and for her enthusiasm and vivacity. In high school she was the cheerleader who thrilled to the successes and wept over the defeats of the team. Not particularly determined on a career direction herself, she was the family "cheerleader" as well and expressed her admiration for her sister and brother who were apparently rather determined achievers with a long list of accomplishments and high aims for their future. S. was sensitive to the problems and moods of her parents and was rewarded by them for her role as "good daughter."

She "naturally" married quite young, shortly after high school, and her marriage was "naturally" to a young man who shared her economic background, religion, and level of education. Being strongly role-oriented, and not particularly ambitious, though a hard worker, her husband quickly settled into a pattern of go to work, come home, eat supper and watch TV, go to bed, have sex twice a week, get up, go to work, etc. He was proud of his ability to fix things and later opened a small fix-it shop in the backyard for the neighborhood trade. Responsibly eager to support his family and satisfied with his routine, he had no feeling that he was missing anything in life. From time to time he was called upon for extra stability, he thought, for his wife had the perplexing tendency to "break down" now and then and was hospitalized several times for depression.

S. found the ongoing years maddeningly dull, but tried to be sensitive to the needs of her husband and growing roster of children, and tried to play the homemaker role with some enthusiasm. When her enthusiasm flagged, it occurred to her that another baby would be nice. Since she was going to be at home anyway, she might as well keep on having kids, was the way she put it. The count got up to eight without any real sense of "planning" for this large number nor for their future needs. S. meantime languished in a cultural wasteland, unstimulated by anything more exciting than the grade school theatricals and the neighborhood drop-ins, who often kept S. on the phone or pouring coffee for hours while they shared their problems with this receptive and adaptive listener. Her intensity muffled, her activity stifled, she envied her sister's unmarried state and interesting life. Over the years her weight climbed and her interest in her appearance dipped, but no one seemed to notice or to care. She sank periodically into periods of weeping and expressed her intensity so dramatically in this way that her well-meaning husband took her to their well-meaning doctor who hospitalized her and "regulated" her on some medication to restore her to a less distressing (for all of them) level of discomfort. Though this was a source of much guilt and shame, she discovered that liquor could blur the acuteness of her discomfort.

Her older daughter's adolescent striving for identity seemed to shake S. into the realization that she had somehow lost her own sense of identity and had become simply an automated role of wife and mother. With painful doubts about the "rightness" of what she was doing, she began to search for a more gratifying life experience and moved into a part-time job, a rigorous weight loss and physical fitness regime, and a search for some of the cultural stimulation available in her community. In the process, she discovered that her husband was unable and unwilling to confirm her outside of her former housewife role and was mystified and hurt that his "blameless" behavior had ended in her dissatisfaction with the marriage. Their marriage, contracted before, or without, any real identification of self and of the way that their temperaments would need closure in the interactive sense, has become one of the dismal statistics in the break-up of The Family. Over the angry protests of her husband, S. has filed for divorce. After identification of her own intense and active temperament dimensions and her talent for getting in touch adaptively with the world around her, she is attempting to use this new knowledge of herself to achieve some sense of gratification. No longer feeling that she must conform to a role of wife and mother that did not recognize her individuality, she has become a vibrant, excited, and exciting woman willing to risk loneliness in search of fulfillment. The attempts of her husband to use custody suits and financial harassment to regain the former status have only served to convince her that she cannot obtain recognition in this marriage.

COMMUNICATION FOR REPAIR

The second and equally important function of communication of one's temperament is for the purpose of "repair" or recuperation. We believe that it is naive and unrealistic to think in terms of having one's life proceed from start to finish without experiencing the "slings and arrows of outrageous fortune." There are no magic formulas, there are no perfect therapies, there is no adequate parenting (or therapeutic reparenting) that will guarantee a life without things going wrong. We all accept this with rueful recognition. Which of us cannot admit with some inward grimace, the truth of Murphy's Law, "Whatever can go wrong, will go wrong"? But even though we recognize this reality, we experience each untoward event as evidence of our own inadequacy or ineptness, as proof that we should have been someone other than who we are and should have done something other than what we did. And in our relationships, we take on the guilt of having failed to be or do what would have avoided the current crisis. So while we think that communication of one's temperament for recognition and confirmation is a positive use of other people in our lives, we think it is just as important a use of relationship to help us repair, restore, or recuperate, when things go wrong.

A useful way of conceptualizing this dual use of relating to others is to borrow the principles and language of systems theory. A system (any system) is a set of elements in interaction and producing an "output" which will be received by the environment. In order for it to operate optimally, it will be necessary to monitor the output and feedback information to the system, so that the system will know when internal changes need to be made. A common example of this feedback loop is the thermostat on the heating system. The thermostat is external to the system and its purpose is to monitor the heat output and refer back the information to the system. If the heat output is within predetermined limits of temperature range, the feedback is negative and the system is "confirmed" in continuing its systemic arrangement. If, or perhaps we should say *when*, the predetermined limits are exceeded, then positive feedback information tells the system that its output is not acceptable and that systemic adjustments should be made to restore or regain its acceptable range.

Translating this simple example into behavioral terms, we can conceptualize an individual as a system that produces behavior (output). For most efficient functioning, such a system would need a reliable feedback loop to reflect back the information about the behavior that was being emitted. It is this need for trusting relationships that can perform this function for us that makes us insist to our group members on the necessity of communicating to others for recognition and for repair. We think of the *confirming response* as being akin to feedback promoting homeostasis which sends the message in effect, "You are being an effective individual and the way you are behaving is acceptable and valued." We think of the *reparative response* as feedback which sends the morphogenetic message, "You are overusing or underusing some element of the system—some adjustment needs to be made for you to be more effective and more acceptable."

This analogy is especially useful because it deals directly with the question of autonomy or self-reliance. As we mentioned earlier, we find our patients especially wary of communicating their temperament because it indicates an "immature" dependence that they have been taught to overcome or outgrow. In addition, they feel that to allow a need for someone else to respond to their behavior is to surrender their autonomy to that other person: "He (or she) would then be taking over and that puts them in charge, not me," is the way we have heard it formulated. Yet the feedback loop in systems terms is *external* to the system and not a part of the internal system itself and the autonomous system must make use of the information in terms of its own potential. To ignore the feedback information is to continue to use one's autonomy in wasteful or self-destructive ways. In fact, failure to get recognition of one's temperament does lead to a kind of hypertrophy of the temperament dimension. For example, if not recognized, the intense person may "escalate" or step-up his intensity, sometimes reaching frenzied proportions which not only are wasteful in the sense of not bringing about the desired response but are also self-destructive in terms of being physically exhausting and debilitating. Even more destructive is the inability to use the response of others as feedback because of the notion that to do so would be to give up one's autonomy. Individuals who have a high level of persistence often find it difficult to take advantage of this feedback information. They fight lonely battles of angry recriminations, with the self-destructive result of isolating themselves.

One of our patients was struggling with the persistence that is the primary temperament component of anorexia nervosa. It was difficult for her to overcome her resistance and continue therapy because even to bring a problem to therapy is in a sense a request for some feedback of information, and she could see that the therapeutic experience itself would possibly be the means by which her behavior could be altered. Remaining in therapy would interfere with *her* control and the expression of her persistence and thus deprive her of her "autonomy." We were able to work with the concept of autonomy as a right to decide what to *do* about information. The autonomous individual herself makes the necessary decisions about her behavior, not by refusing to allow communication from others, but by seeking trusting relationships and asking for the feedback. Without such feedback the Persister does not know when she has exceeded limits and will continue in ways that are wasteful and destructive.

Case of Lack of Repair—Mrs. P.

One of the style clusters that we find particularly in need of recognition and repair from close relationships is the Intenser whose strong expression of feeling is often experienced by others as unwelcome, disturbing, or downright threatening. Often these people learn in childhood that they are overwhelming to others and may be the recipients of strong disciplinary action or much disapproval, particularly around any negative feelings such as anger or scared or sad feelings. Consequently, they learn to suppress unacceptable feelings or displace them onto scapegoats. In some cases, there is a "somatizing" of intensity that can be experienced in a variety of bodily sensations.

One such Intenser was Mrs. P., a 40-year-old woman whose marriage to a lawyer had become a long-smoldering battleground of vindictive sorties and had erupted into a warfare that "threatened her sanity" and prompted suicidal thoughts. Although she had been thought of as a joyous, gay and free child and young woman and had received recognition for rather intense expressions of enjoyment, her family had promoted the idea that feelings of distress were not acceptable. Her mother, a weak, wan woman, seemed to need protection and shielding from life's discomforts, and the family carried on a rather make-believe life of gaiety and good manners, carefully avoiding the "ugliness" of life. In her adult life she continued this pattern of trying to shut out any recognition of problems or any intrusion of difficulties, preferring to surround herself with "beautiful" people and a schedule of "lovely" social engagements. Her marriage to a successful man had the flaw of his having come from a lower class background whose way of life was "disgusting" to her.

In the early years of marriage, she suffered the profoundly real trauma of the fatal illness of a little daughter. During the two years of this illness, Mrs. P. fought strongly against accepting the pain of this situation and often played make-believe games of pretending that the child was normal like others. She never allowed herself to talk about her predicament and even at the child's funeral tried not to appear grieved. In recounting this behavior, she stated that, "People do not want to be bothered with the depressing feelings of others."

Over the years she has engaged in numerous skirmishes with her husband and two children around behavior she found personally distressing. Her husband's continuing close relations with his parents were a constant source of argument. With her children she either tried to overprotect and shield them from discomfort or met their problems with suppressive shouting. Everyone in her family was constantly blamed for "making her feel bad"; she came to therapy wanting to know what to do to change them and stop their distressing behavior. As with so many Intensers, she felt that others should be aware of her sensitivity and behave accordingly. She should not have to tell anyone what she was feeling. Not being able to communicate her own feelings of grief and sadness so as to receive recognition and comfort from others, she has felt angry and outraged when those around her have brought their negative feelings to her attention. Her husband's reaction to her intense expressions of anger was an attempt to reason with her and explain to her that her feelings were irrational; he thus deprived her of the satisfactory closure of acceptance and caused her to step up the frenzy of her anger. She described her physical reactions at such times as a sensation of "filling up" to the point where she felt she could "explode."

These family battles continued until she became physically exhausted, emotionally depressed, and suicidal. It became apparent to us that what she really wanted was to be able to bring up the fact that she had distressing feelings for which she needed repair. But in order to communicate this need, she had to first identify herself as the source of her intense feelings and stop seeings others as responsible for producing and handling her feelings. Only then could she begin to accept the full scope of her own intensity. Accepted by the group as an Intenser and encouraged to recognize the fact that intensity involves *all* feelings, she began to communicate her sadness (and the anger over lack of recognition of these feelings from those close to her). With such recognition from others, she could then accept the behavior of others as based on *their* temperament dimensions and life situations and not constructed to make her feel badly. There was then no longer a need to use her in-laws as scapegoats or to try to "shut out" the "ugly" world outside her door.

COMMUNICATION FOR CONFIRMATION AND SUPPORT

Another example serves to show how yet another style cluster can experience the lack of recognition and repair that could become available through communication to others in interpersonal networks. The Doer is a cluster that often needs recognitional support. The Doer receives the gratifying sense of closure from active completion of a task, but there is a normal accompanying affect of anxiety about the outcome. This is not necessarily a fear of failure but more of an anxiety about whether he is proceeding correctly toward successful completion.

A Case of Lack of Confirmation and Support

One Doer we treated was a 28-year-old divorced woman who came for therapy because she felt at the end of her rope trying to juggle a demanding job, taking care of two small children, and finding satisfactory heterosexual relationships. She was experiencing herself as peculiarly depersonalized—losing more and more contact with herself and seriously considering suicide. She had experienced exploitation from childhood on. Her parents had divorced early in her life, and she saw herself as taking care of many of her mother's problems. Her mother was a complaining, critical person who was quick to blame her life discomforts on others. Our patient tried hard to never disappoint her; she was a particularly good student who worried but never turned to her mother for support. Her father was an egocentric person who gathered attention for himself but never seemed to spontaneously notice his daughter's achievements. One way in which she had often been exploited was by having to ask her father to mail in the child support funds. Her husband was unaware of her feelings and expected her to be completely available for him in what she saw as his "macho" style. Her subsequent relationships with men, after her divorce, were also marked by her meeting their sexual needs and she saw men as mostly exploitive and demanding. Though she tried in innumerable ways to please, she was rarely rewarded with their concern for her.

Prior to seeing us, she had accepted a job as one of the first women to assume a supervisory position in a "heavy industry" factory. She was apparently selected to break into this former all-male situation, in compliance with "affirmative action" policies of the company, not only because of her known competence but because of her ability to please others and not be "demanding" for herself. She was seen as less "threatening" to male sensitivities than a woman who would be assertive. She was warned by her superior that she would have to supervise without being "tough" or "unladylike," which would antagonize her superiors, co-workers, and the group of men she was in charge of. She did exceedingly well in learning her job, but was continually anxious about the possibility that she might not know something that she "should" know. She endured sexist harassment and innuendoes, ranging from stories that she had been given the job because she "slept with the boss" to having workers address her familiarly in a way they would never have dared to speak to a male supervisor. She suffered the internal accusation that she was not being a good mother to her two children because of the long hours of overtime work that her job required.

Her style cluster was that of a Doer with a strong component of adaptiveness, and we felt that she was not recognizing either her style or the accompanying affect of anxiety about successful outcomes. She used her adaptive quickness to quickly grasp the essentials of her job and was sensitive also to the feelings of being threatened that lay behind much of the harassment that she experienced. But like many who are quick to adapt, her own feelings and needs could easily get ignored while she attempted to do what others seemed to be requiring of her. Without the self-recognition of her own style, she was unable to ask for *confirmation* of herself as a hard worker and for *support* for continuing to work toward mastery of the situation. She needed to recognize how her temperamental tendencies to work hard toward her goal (her high level of activity) and to be always aware of pressures from others (her quick-to-adapt dimensions) were being overused or hypertrophied without the feedback of information from others.

THE IMPORTANCE OF COMMUNICATION, A REPRISE

It has been our experience that the communication of one's temperament is the crucial element in the application of theories of temperament in adult life. The identification of temperament dimensions and the further identity of one's style cluster are, of course, the base on which the theory rests. We have accepted the evidence from the New York Longitudinal Study that such temperament dimensions are present and can be identified early in life. We have further become convinced that these early-identified dimensions persist through stages of growth and that they may be manifested in different ways and under varying pressures from the socializing process as well as by the process of growth and development.

But the presence and persistence of temperament can only remain an interesting "fact" of individuality, until or unless there is some way to incorporate this fact into the conscious ego-identity and to communicate this identity to others. It is in the process of communication that the self-identity becomes complete, becomes recognized by others, and is reflected back to the individual. The individual must continue the process of communication of himself throughout life or suffer the painful experience of isolation. Thus, the task of establishing gratifying relationships can be accomplished only by presenting one's identity for recognition to others.

In adults we find many relationships stunted by limited and guarded communication. Since many of our interactions are themselves limited and contractual, our incomplete communication of ourselves can be masked by role-defined and socially acceptable behavior. Yet such relationships are not sufficient to bring us the satisfaction of being understood and valued for who we are.

Interactive trust, the daring to present or disclose our identity to another for his recognition, is not easily come by. Our vulnerability is on the line when we disclose our identity to others for their confirmation or our need for their reparative help when things go wrong. If there were another way to assure ourselves of recognition of our own personal value, of the support of others toward our life goals, or of the assistance we need when things go wrong, we would use it. But we can think of no other way.

Part IV

Uses of Temperament Counseling

12

Temperament in Psychotherapy

GOALS IN THERAPY

Although our earliest interest in temperament stemmed from our insistent search for a way to think of mental illness in terms of a preventative model, we have become interested in the application of our concepts about temperament to the problems presented by people who come to us for psychotherapy.

In the course of our personal involvement, both as patients and as therapists, we had become aware of the centrality of change as a therapeutic goal. One did not present oneself for therapy if one was satisfied with oneself; one came because of self-dissatisfaction. The assumption was that the well-motivated patient wanted to change who he was and become who he could or should be. Dynamically-oriented therapists, armed with the tools to strip back resistances, saw themselves as the surgeons for change. There seemed to be a tendency to question any behavior which seemed deviant from the accepted structure, and to view the person involved in such behavior as the victim of unresolved conflicts which could be altered by the therapeutic process. Thus, a woman wanting a divorce from other than a wife-beating, alcoholic husband was seen as mentally suspect; surely she must be depressed, or manic, or stuck in the maws of an unresolved oedipal conflict. Children with developmental irregularity or rebelliousness must be suffering from some internal neurotic problem or from defective parenting. Women wanting to work outside their middle-class home must be into some significant denial. Men not succeeding in their work had some serious ego defect in identification. Students doing poorly in school or flunking out of college should be whisked off to psychotherapy. All of these situations cried out for change; we could all change if we would only stop resisting.

In the social upheavals and rapid changes in what is considered normative in our society, definitions of acceptable and deviant behavior also changed. It is no longer usual to consider the woman who decides to divorce as a candidate for psychotherapeutic intervention nor the unmarried young woman who elects to live with a man as rebelliously acting out. The decision to protest the Vietnam war by political pressure and draft resistance was a position of many young people who, though they differed with the official position of their government, were not sick or pathological. The eruptions of the Civil Rights Movement and the Women's Movement have made it clear that, although old roles are discarded and new demands are made, the individuals who espouse these causes are not pathologically deviant; they want to be free to be themselves. In such a rapidly changing society, people are becoming aware of the exquisite nature of individuality and are beginning to see themselves and others as who they *are* and have the right to be, not who they should be or regretted not being.

Even so, changes in society come about unevenly. There are still many people whose way of behaving seems out of harmony with their own expectations of what they think of as "right" behavior, and many more who are seen by those close to them as behaving unacceptably or in ways that need therapeutic attention. Sometimes, also, the new freedom of behavior is not something that earlier socialization allows us to readily accept and the loss of role structure and expected responses from others causes emotional distress. Our premise, that any temperament style is acceptable since it is an inherent factor, is not totally true for the society at large. As we mentioned earlier, we see a larger than expected number of women in therapy whom we consider Intensers. We hypothesize that women Intensers may have difficulty getting confirmation and support since intensity of expression is not a valued component for the role of wife and mother. The man Intenser is not so disapproved of and the man who expresses himself with emphasis and strength, even anger and aggression, is tolerated and sometimes valued for his "forceful-ness." We find a larger than expected proportion of male With-drawer-Controllers in our therapy groups who present themselves as threatened by the changes which are going on all about them and who feel they are struggling to "regain control" which they sense is being taken from them. Women Withdrawers are not as threat-ened. Again, we hypothesize that it is preferable to many men *and* women that women remain in the old role structures. Many women, even those who are actively moving ahead in career development and freer life styles, protest that they do not like the changes they see occurring all around them: a woman who has fought for the right to be a telephone lineworker or a truck driver protests, "But I'm not one of those women's libbers!"; a college woman preparing for a professional career protests her femininity by wanting her date to pay for their evening's entertainment or to gallantly light her ciga-rette and hold open doors for her.

The more pluralistic view of acceptable individualism has led us to think of psychotherapy as being no longer guided by societal goals. Our approach to therapy is anchored in our firm acceptance of the inherent presence and the continued persistence into adult life of dimensions of temperament. Even though we can see that behavior may be altered by the way in which one's individuality is recognized and encouraged, or denied and repressed, we also see the tempera-ment that underlies behavior as unchangeable. Therefore, our ther-apy is no longer directed toward the idea of changing patients. Our therapeutic goal becomes one of acceptance of oneself through iden-tification of one's temperamental style and finding ways to more fully enter into effective temperamental interaction with others. In our attempts to help people get in touch with dimensions of their temperament and bring this to a conscious level, we are trying to bring their style of behaving more clearly to mind so that they can present this knowledge of themselves to others for their recognition and confirmation.

It is in the lack of such conscious recognition of temperament that we see the origins of much behavior in social interactions that can result at best in ungratifying relationships, and at worst in behavior that can be considered pathological and in need of therapeutic intervention. While the person who has come to terms with the temperament style that is manifested in how he behaves can communicate this to others for their interactive support, the person who is unaware of his temperament style may *unconsciously* become victimized by overusing dimensions of his temperament to produce behavior that is considered pathological. It is this overuse or hypertrophy of temperament that we see as putting the individual out of harmony with himself or with his environment. We see these people as living lives of dissonance, of not being in touch with the productive use of their temperament, and as suffering the pain of non-acceptance of themselves. In their inability to establish consonant relationships with others and to reach a sense of gratification that we refer to as "closure," we find that people tend to repeat or escalate their behavior towards others with the hope of gaining recognition. Unfortunately this hypertrophied expression of temperament produces further dissonance.

Using our six style clusters as useful examples of the way this process is carried out, we believe we can see some interesting counterparts to the pathological designations that are used in traditional therapies. In the style cluster that we call the *Persister* (which includes the dimensions of high level of persistence, slowness to adapt, a rather negative quality of mood, and sometimes a fairly high amount of distractibility), we find that non-recognition or non-acceptance of this style by others can result in fears of being thwarted and interrupted and a consequent unwillingness to receive interactive input. In order to reject this input, the behavior becomes a largely repetitive presentation that tends to become stylized and ritualized. It is an activity carried out for its own sake only, never leading to any closure. In this way, the Persister's excessive behavior resembles the classical obsessive-compulsive set of symptoms, the intention of which is to ward off bad behavior, punishment, or evil consequences. In our formulation we see the repetitive behavior as warding off interactive acceptance, reassurance, and information. Our Persisters are recognizable in their failure to accept from others any signals of "enoughness" since they interpret this as a threat to their autonomy.

The person who uses to excess the style cluster which we call *Withdrawer* or *Withdrawer-Controller* (which includes also a low or selective quality of mood, middle to high intensity, slowness to adapt, and rhythmicity or regularity) experiences new situations with anxiety and responds with much avoidance behavior. The Withdrawer in need of therapy appears suspicious and negative. He takes even accidental mishaps as threatening and plans ways to "get even" or "regain control." He is always on the lookout for danger or unwanted outcomes. In this way his behavior resembles the pathological symptoms of the paranoid individual and he appears somewhat phobic in his need to be constantly on guard against a menacing world.

When the *Intenser* is denied recognition and acceptance, his escalation of intensity, which is used to express both positive and negative feelings and moods, may bear a marked resemblance to the behavior labeled hysterical or manic-depressive in the more traditional nomenclature. As the expression of feelings is emphasized, with "highs" and "lows" being dramatically expressed, the Intenser can readily seem pathological to less intense individuals. We find the intense person and his or her spouse ready to consider this hypertrophy as "crazy" and in need of "treatment" or medication. The heightened sensitivity to bodily sensations, which many Intensers report, suggests the hysterias described in the earlier literature.

The *Approacher*, with his high approach, quickness to adapt, low threshold of response, and tendency toward distractibility, appears to be waiting for stimulation from others. Without conscious recognition of this temperament style and some interactive help in keeping it within reasonable bounds, Approachers can appear to have loose ego identity and some loss of ego boundaries. It is as if they do not know who they are or what they need or want, but pick up on whatever presents itself. They sometimes appear vague, limp, and "mushy." One young woman Approacher, when asked to tell her group what her objectives were in coming to group therapy, shrugged her shoulders and said vaguely that she didn't know.

The *Adapter,* that pleasant companion, can sometimes extend his adaptiveness to such a point that he cannot adapt to the many diverse personalities or situations that present themselves. Without interactive support towards limiting the demands he feels he must meet, the Adapter may withdraw to a private world while still outwardly trying to adapt to others. In his need to gain some surcease from the high costs of continuous adapting, he may resort to alcoholism or other adddictive behavior. We have observed other Adapters whose retreat takes the form of excessive sleeping or indulging in a daydream world that approaches the delusional.

The *Doer,* whose achievement and productiveness are so valued in our society, may experience the costs of his temperament in terms of simple anxiety over the possibility of failure or, if failure does occur for any reason, in terms of overwhelming reactive depression. The Doer who has interactive recognition and support can use his anxiety profitably to "psych" himself into action and accomplishment. Without these he can *overuse* his anxiety so that it gets turned around into ways that will keep him from doing. One of our adult Doers remembers that as a child she would faint when she felt she couldn't grasp something new in her schoolwork. Another remembers crying so piteously that she would be sent home from school. This woman, in fact, is working in therapy on ways to communicate her anxiety about her ability to master her goals. In this way she can use the recognition and support of others to move her ahead in her musical career. Her obvious talent needs further training and discipline, but her anxiety about whether she can succeed keeps her from taking the steps to accomplish this.

We have worked with all of these types of problems in our application of temperament to psychotherapy, thereby supporting our own conviction that there is no guaranteed trouble-free temperament style and that any one of us can find ourselves in need of therapeutic help from time to time. Therapy as we see it is not a tool of the society to bring its "deviants" back into line or to underwrite the institutionalized behavior that is currently normative. Rather, therapy should serve to restore and support the sense of individuality so necessary for the effective functioning which is the hallmark of mental health. In order to achieve our goals of enhancing individuality and using the interactive experiences of adult life towards the achievement of gratifying closure, we have developed a system of dealing with temperament from a threefold position: 1) temperament self-identification and acceptance; 2) communication to others for confirmation and repair; and, 3) recognition of others' temperament.

Because our approach to counseling was first a non-judgmental identification of each individual's style, we soon discovered that we had stopped seeing patients in terms of pathological signs. We essentially no longer think of our non-psychotic patients as sick people or disordered people; rather we see them as living an interactive life that is dissonant with their style. Our approach is to help them become aware of this and to effectively proceed to a consonance with their style. Our uses of their history are for: 1) further evidence for identification of temperament dimensions; 2) some understanding of the courses of dissonance and of the attempts to modify these dimensions.

We soon stopped our search for antecedent causes in behavior. We found that one of the basic resistances to identification and self-acceptance of temperament lay in the persistent search for *why!* Most of our patients, either through their exposure to current psychodynamic thinking about uncovering the basic traumatic features of childhood or for other developmental reasons, felt that their therapeutic success or progress depended on as yet not sufficiently understood reasons that would mysteriously explain all.

Temperament, by virtue of its designation as given, and by concerning itself with "how," becomes a point of useful departure toward the single question, *"How are you going to live your life?"*

With the above in mind, we see our therapy as an educational procedure (threefold, as stated before) that can serve as an alternative structure to conventional therapy.

1. Temperament Identification

We found empirically that certain procedures seemed more effective than others. In general, group therapy seems to offer more than individual therapy. Our first activity is to proceed with self-identification of temperament style. In an individual session we explain something about our theories, our dependency on the prior work of Thomas and Chess with children, and our thoughts as to why this could be helpful. Then we give the patient some reading material we have prepared, further enlarging the concept of adult temperament, and ask him to fill out a simple, selective, self-rating questionnaire (Appendix A). He brings this questionnaire back for the second session. At this time, by the process of collating the patient's self-observations, our clinical observations, and the answers to questions calculated to get further historical and elucidative validation, we proceed to a first effort at identification, and one that might have to be changed as we go on in therapy. It is apparent that very few people think of themselves in terms of temperament. We use our extrapolations of the nine dimensions proposed for children by Thomas-Chess and we often find that we bring up dimensions which people have never considered about themselves. We are struck by the alacrity with which almost everyone grasps the process and appreciates this view of himself. First of all, we are non-judgmental— there are no superior-inferior dimensions. We are able to point out the equal place of all temperament dimensions in our social life. Secondly, many of these people have been characterized by others as "crazy" or "sick" for a number of years of their life, and many have accepted that there is indeed something "wrong" with them. For the first time, they experience a sense of acceptance as they really are. One can almost see the labels slipping away and the attendant relief.

We then work with our patient in identifying a particular combination of dimensions which can be seen as his style cluster. The six style clusters which we have identified as typical enable the individual to quickly grasp the concept of style and with few exceptions we find the patient can identify himself as approximating one of the six. For example, to call a person an Intenser emphasizes the primacy of expressing feelings in a heightened manner (heightened, that is, in comparison with more usual expressions when the same or similar situations present themselves to other people). A person who is an Intenser may also be a very highly active person and may feel that doing is as important as feeling and expressing feelings in his way of reacting. Usually we can work with both styles in helping the individual recognize his temperament. However, we do not find one person displaying two contradictory styles. The Adapter will not be a Withdrawer or a Persister, for example.

Not too many are fully comfortable about claiming their temperament style, but armed with this tentative identification of himself, our patient is introduced to the group with whom he will be working during his therapy.

We generally try to move all of our individual patients into group therapy unless there is some adamant objection to it or unless they are undergoing severe stress and crisis. In such cases, individual therapy continues until the crisis situation is better controlled before group therapy is initiated. There is often some resistance to group work, particularly if the individual is a Withdrawer who seems to fear group interaction and exposure more than those with other temperament sytles. The Withdrawer, in a way that we have learned to recognize and expect, will usually handle his anxiety over this new situation by a sort of hairsplitting, argumentative, querulous, and sometimes outrightly diminishing approach. This can easily be experienced as controlling intimidation, but we find that if we stay with the Withdrawer, recognizing his fears and encouraging him to try this new experience, he will sooner or later let go of control and come along. (We have to admit it is sometimes tempting to withdraw from a Withdrawer.) Intensers also usually are frightened at the prospect of group "exposure," but easily break into interaction once they have become a part of a group.

Although recognition and identification often have a positive effect on a patient, we find that it is easy to slip back into the habitual framework of the *non-identified* state. Therefore, we send out a summary newsletter of every meeting to each group member. The newsletter restates what was said in group, again identifies the temperament style we saw in interaction, and gives us a chance to add any further thoughts we have had since the session. We see this as an effective reinforcement between sessions and also a kind of developmental history of therapy that one can turn to later. This newsletter is our clinical record; there is nothing added.

2. *Temperament Communication*

The second step, communication for confirmation, usually involves presenting one's identity to another for his recognition and acceptance. We see this as a need for ratifying one's autonomy and as asking for support from another. This support can be a simple assent to the identification. ("I understand that you are an Intense person," or, "I recognize that you need time before feeling at ease about this new situation.") It can also be actual encouragement to do something in spite of resistances against taking action. As stated before, the Doer needs support in the face of fears of non-success, the Withdrawer needs encouragement in the face of the desire to hold back, the Adapter needs support exhibiting his own creativity, the Intenser needs the reassurance that expressing feelings will not "sound crazy." The support that is needed may also be some stimulation toward closure. The Approacher can use this stimulation to motivate himself into action. The Persister can use a reminder that he can round off and complete an activity, if he has been able to communicate to another his need for this sort of supportive interaction. Patients are encouraged to see their special need for interactive communication. We believe there is no true autonomy without interactive help. This is never fully incorporated from one's childhood but needs renewing over and over again.

Communication for repair is the interactive response to the inevitable occurrence of dissonance. With each temperament style, carrying out one's behavior can also lead to unrewarding consequences. The individual will need to recuperate his sense that he is still acceptable and valuable and that the way he acts is the way that is right for him. For example, the Doer gets ample reward in our society since we offer much admiration for productiveness and accomplishments. However, the Doer cannot always remain a stranger to failure to achieve his goals. The saying that if you have never failed at anything you probably haven't tried much may be true, but it doesn't do much for the person who is currently facing the depression of failure. What is needed is the empathic response of recognition of the depressed feelings over lack of success and the heightened anxiety about further effort. But in addition, repair for the Doer again recognizes that activity (doing) is the way that this person works for gratification. The encouragement to use this dimension of temperament to evaluate the situation and make further decisions helps the Doer to recover his feelings of consonance.

In sum, reparative communication seems to have three parts: 1) recognition and empathy for the dissonant situation; 2) recognition of the individual's temperament style as a part of the dissonant situation (through overuse, for example) ; and, 3) support towards a more consonant use of the temperament style. In this way the individual can again recover his value for himself as a person with a given temperament style even while he recognizes the need to take this style into account in his behavior.

Another example may serve to clarify this process. S.I., to whom we referred as an example of occupational dissonance in Chapter 10; is an Adapter. He led his agency in a sales job where his friendly adaptiveness received almost daily recognition. Reminiscent of the "Peter Principle," in which a person doing well in one job is promoted to a higher status positon where his talents are not necessarily fitting, S.I. was put in charge of an administrative job where he was caught in the middle between two opposing factions. Unable to use his adaptiveness productively, since adapting to one faction meant antagonizing the other, S.I. still tried to adaptively appear to be going along with both. The ensuing impasse convinced him he was not "man enough" to carry the new job. He found himself extremely fatigued, found himself "mumbling" when he tried to talk to his co-workers, finally became aware of a "heart condition" of rapid and pounding heart beats. The reparative work with S.I., after identification of his Adaptive temperament style, was to empathically recognize the way his tendency to adapt to others led him into this overuse of his temperament style. The group helped him recognize that the "promotion" had deprived him of the productive use of his temperament by not allowing the creative use of his ability to be in touch with the needs of his customers. He later asked for and received a transfer back to the former position.

3. *Temperament Recognition in Others*

The third step in using temperament therapy is to help the individual recognize the temperament of others. Consonant parent-child interactions rest upon the ability and the willingness for the parent to identify and accept the temperament of his child, so that the child is socialized and parented through various stages of growth and development with his temperament known and respected. Such early recognition and support of temperament provide the foundation for successful and consonant adult interactions.

We are not speaking here of the superficial interactions or the casual and limited interactions which can remain dictated by custom, "manners," or contracts. The interactions which we are dealing with are rather those of one's "primary" groups and include those people with whom we are in ongoing, face-to-face, and meaningful (i.e., important to us) relationships. This would include a wide variety of relationships, foremost among which would be one's "immediate" family, one's primary work group, and/or one's circle of intimates. It is in this network that roles and habitual expectations of others become real barriers to recognizing and accepting individuality. Holding on to ideas of behavior as determined by the norms for a particular role stifles individuality and creates a socially structured relationship. We find our patients making such statements as, "A wife doesn't say that to a husband." "Children don't tell mothers; mothers tell children." "You can't say that to a boss." All of these statements indicate they are not looking at these people as individuals, but as people playing roles which carry with them a set of expected behaviors. It is an important part of therapy to help people to begin to recognize the temperament styles of others and to be able to respond to others in terms of their individuality.

As anyone who has ever participated in group therapy knows, groups become very quickly the sort of groups we all recognize as "primary." Weekly sessions and permission to disclose personal problems quickly foster a feeling of caring closeness among group members. In our groups, the purpose is steadily turned toward identification of temperament and the communication of this knowledge of oneself for recognition and repair. It is in this exchange that our patients become consciously aware, many of them for the first time, of their individuality and the individual style of others. Now each individual must be considered. "Who is he?" becomes, "How does he display himself?" "How does he react to situations and people?" "How does he relate to others and to his life experiences?" With our emphasis on style, we have seen our group members recognize one another in new ways, openly identify for each other their tendency to withdraw, to react intensely, to persist, and so forth. With this recognition, the group gives the individual the chance to consciously decide how to make use of this knowledge of the way others see his or her temperament style.

In addition to the interaction in group meetings, we reinforce this knowledge in our after-group notes to patients. These notes, mentioned earlier as a way to assist in the process of self-identification, are also useful in helping patients to become more consciously aware of the temperament styles of others in the group.

Two Examples of Therapeutic Application of Temperament Concepts

In an earlier chapter (p. 114), we described a marriage situation which involved a Withdrawer husband and a wife who was very much a Doer. This particular combination is frequently a "difficult fit" in marriage partners, as is also the combination of Withdrawer and Intenser. Because we felt this marriage to be at a particularly difficult juncture, we elected to treat the two marriage partners as separate therapy patients, hoping to allow each to come to grips with his or her particular temperament style and how this style was being displayed in all interactions, before we tried to do any marriage counseling with them. Following is a treatment history showing the way we worked with this husband in group therapy and some idea of how we tried to bring about our goals of identification, communication and recognition of others.

Case of T.B.

T.B. was a 35-year-old man who came to therapy with severe marital and family problems. He felt himself to be the victim of irrational people around him, particularly his wife. His main purpose in coming to therapy was to get some expert advice as to how he could handle her more effectively and put some sense in her head. As this was initially presented to us, it had a peculiar ring of coldness, matter-of-factness, and finality. We were struck by the dimension of his temperament we were later to identify as non-adaptive. He seemed not to be able to get in touch with someone else's feelings and made peculiarly distorted assessments of others' feelings. He also displayed a "nitpicking" argumentativeness and engaged us in long dialogues before he could signify his acceptance of any of our concepts. As therapists, we experienced a ense of alienated nonacceptance, and it took a certain therapeutic dedication to pursue our interaction with him. In our first few sessions, he was able to convey his fearfulness of new social situations. But what kept us most involved with him was our awareness of his personal pain which was covered over with attacking behavior. His preemptive demanding behavior actually was his response to his feeling hurt—but who could know it!

Our first task was to proceed with identification of his temperament dimensions and the problem of which dimension to emphasize first. T.B.'s self-rating questionnaire made it apparent that he functioned most decidedly in the Withdrawer style cluster. This was explained to him and, as with most Withdrawers, we had to deal simply with the pejorative sense of the word "withdrawal." In American culture, to be a Withdrawer is almost an unforgivable sin. The implications of the Dale Carnegie concept and the recent growth of "shyness clinics" attest to our cultural disapproval of any evidence of withdrawal. We told T.B. that Withdrawers have the natural tendency to respond to all new situations with a feeling of anxious discomfort and an initial movement toward withdrawal. T.B. could finally acknowledge that he questioned everything initially and "tested out" new situations and people. He had perceived that others were often irritated by this initial oppositionality, and had interpreted this response from others as meaning that he was not wanted or accepted. He was pleasantly surprised that we could stay with him until he had worked through his first oppositional reactions.

As T.B. accepted his withdrawal dimension, we were able then to help him identify other aspects of his style cluster. His low quality of mood seemed to fit in with his expectancy that others would reject him and that new situations were not to be trusted. To go beyond this expectancy would be to become very vulnerable and to risk experiencing some hurt. For the Withdrawer, with his quickness to retreat, the awareness of this painfully tender feeling can get lost and he seems insensitive to his own or to others' vulnerability. Sometimes unbelievably hurting things can be spoken by him to others with no apparent recognition of how they sound to those others. He handles his own vulnerability in two ways: one way is to simply have very little to do with the world around him and to communicate as little as necessary; the other is to engage in some controlling action toward others. This controllingness becomes expressed in supercritical demands on others. People living with Withdrawers complain that not only are they never praised, but they constantly feel as if they haven't done enough or done anything just right.

In addition to controlling by being highly critical, the Withdrawer often attempts to control the activities of others in the family and will want to say where they can go, with whom, and for how long they can be gone. Eventually, this leads to rebellion of those controlled, although this rebellion may come only after a long period of uncomplaining trying. We began in group and in our group notes to openly refer to his temperament style cluster as "Withdrawer-Controller" and, again, had to deal with the pejorative meaning of "controllingness." We saw this need to control others as a way to give himself some time to get in touch with all the possibilities of what might go wrong. We feel that this is basically because of the slow-to-adapt dimension of the Withdrawer. The issue of control was noted again and again as T.B. told about his interactions with his wife and children and finally he began to see how his demandingness appeared to others.

When T.B. had been able to accept his temperament style cluster as Withdrawer-Controller, we could begin to point out the possibility of using someone's standby encouragement toward moving gradually beyond his initial withdrawal stance. If a Withdrawer can decide to trust another person with the knowledge that he is fearful of new situations, he can also admit his need for their encouragement and acceptance of his pace of entry into action. As the group members began to identify for him their awareness of the hurt feelings behind the blustering controlling statements that he reported about his home interactions, T.B.'s first response was a kind of mystified blinking of his eyes as if he were trying to see something hazily off in the distance. At first he didn't know what we were talking about. He was not aware of feeling anything other than anger and the need to demand compliance from those around him. Only slowly did his hurt feelings, and his tears, appear, along with his shocked awareness that he had never recognized these feelings. He slowly but definitely claimed and expressed their presence in his life and received recognition and confirmation from the group. He could now communicate his need for repair and begin to recover from this painful isolation of himself from others. The special need of the Withdrawer is for a relationship with someone who is adaptive enough to be aware of his often carefully concealed fears and to provide this information to him. As a rule, a crucial constancy of relationship is necessary. The group offered this to T.B. by not backing away from his alienating attempts to control us.

In his continued participation in group sessions, T.B. began to become aware of the differences in other people. He continued to blink with surprise to realize that persons with other temperament styles were not concerned with keeping control or figuring out in advance what things could possibly go wrong. He responded to an Adapter in our group with, "Why should you care what that person thinks? You know what should be done," and to a Doer with, "You mean that you worry about how you would feel if something you were doing failed? All you need to know is what your alternatives would be." He did, in fact, begin to see that these temperamental styles were as "right" as his own position of cautious control and that others were as much in need of confirmation, support, and encouragement from those close to them as his wife and children had been. The continued emphasis on recognizing individuality in the group sessions has been helpful to T.B., not to change him, but to give him a different perspective about himself and about his interactions with others.

Case of N.

The case of N. presents a quite different temperament style. N. is a 40-year-old woman who came to therapy because she was unable to bring to an end a lengthy affair which jeopardized not only her family stability but her personal integrity, as well. She felt substantially out of control and alarmingly sensed herself as verging on "craziness" and possibly suicide. She recalled that from early childhood her usual role had been to be the intermediary who pleased others or helped them settle their differences amicably. She lived until marriage with her divorced mother who was a lady of "gentle upbringing" and who was mystified by her husband's wish for a divorce. This lady transmitted the values of her own socialization to her daughter, dressing her prettily, being sure that she had "proper" activities, and discouraging her interest in roughhouse games in the neighborhood.

N. married a widower who was quite a bit older than herself and who had one child from a previous marriage. Their family increased with the birth of their son. Together they worked and saved money, N. working as a highly valued secretary in an investment company. As they became more affluent, they moved to a better address in the suburbs, and discovered new standards of dress, transportation, recreation, and even sexuality. N. described herself as being inundated by these social expectations of her new friends, and she felt strong discomfort in attempting to resist their blandishments.

The sexual arrangement in their marriage was one of almost rare encounters with little dash or sophistication on the part of either. It was as if they had decided this was not going to be their field of expertise. Eventually, N. succumbed to a rather artful lover who effectively combined his macho qualities with a plaintive helplessness that could not long be denied. It turned into a furious affair, carried basically by his sexual attraction to her, while she struggled to construct the proper responses of the mistress. He eventually tired of his role, so that she began experiencing herself as less pleasing to him. She intensified her attempts to please, engaging in behavior quite erratic and perilous to her marriage. Any hint of his need for her brought her running. Her inability to keep from spending herself in this way finally led to her coming to therapy.

After some individual therapy sessions, we suggested that N. join one of our groups. N. was a very attractive woman, impeccably dressed in fashionable "name" styles from expensive stores and with a style that was slighlty exhibitionistic. Her clothes and accessories were often the subject of the animated chitchat before group sessions began. In the sessions she took an active role. Although usually fairly quiet in the group about her own reasons for being there, she displayed a strong adaptive response to others, often sensitively probing their feelings or offering empathic recognition. Her own self-effacing and apologetic remarks were somewhat infiltrated by sadness. She displayed what appeared to be a high level of activity. She could usually recount a week's schedule that was packed with one event after another and included not only her own activities but the activities she had planned for her daughter, her relatives and her friends, all of whom seemed to depend upon her. We thought of her as an Adapter. Her apparent "doingness" was almost always involved

with doing for others rather than being used to bring her gratification for her own accomplishments. Often she would miss
sessions because of others' "demands" on her.

Although she felt she was capable of advancement to investment counselor rank at her job, she so perfectly fulfilled the role
of thoughtfully taking care of her boss' office that it was apparent
she had made herself indispensable as the "perfect secretary."
She was careful not to flaunt her capabilities too obviously and
would often correct the work of other secretaries without telling
them. She was happy for others even as she saw them given
opportunities for which she would have wanted to be considered.
The group gave her active support towards working for closure
for herself, although she herself did not solicit this support. Her
tales of her excessive generosity towards others always prompted
the group members to react with anger that she was being "used"
and exploited by others. Although she thanked us nicely for our
solicitousness, she rarely followed through with the group's
pointed advice.

Eventually the affair was ended, whether due to her action
or her lover's drift to a new provider we were never sure. She
made some gains in asserting her own needs for accomplishment,
enrolling in some college courses and managing to do for herself
without first piling up a week's worth of doing for others in order
to feel alright about it. She was unable to communicate either
to the group or to her husband what she found deficient in her
married life or what recognition and support she needed from
others.

In terms of recognition of others, although she was friendly,
empathic, and solicitous of others in the group and was well
liked by them in return, we did not hear statements that really
recognized them as individuals; rather she saw them as objects
to whom she could bring some help.

She still seems to think of her husband and children as recipients of her willingness to adapt to their wants. The pursuit of
her own interests remains covert lest it be criticized as unnecessary and interfering. She left therapy with many thanks for the
upsurge of confidence in herself and she felt she had regained the
control that she had lost for a while in her impetuous affair.
We see this as an unfinished result but are not without hope
that our stress on recognition and communication of her individuality will be of some help as she continues to work out
her life choices.

13

Temperament in
Family Counseling

In several earlier chapters we have mentioned marital and family interaction in our development of concepts of temperament in adult interaction. When we discussed the fits of two adult temperaments, we spoke of the different types of spouses and how these might end in either consonant or dissonant marriages. When we discussed communication, we used marriages as prime examples of the importance of communication for recognition and support. Again, when we described our methods of working with temperament theory in adult therapy, problems in marriages were often primary sources of the interactive difficulty which brought the individual to therapy. In all of these instances, we were focusing on the individual in the marriage. In this chapter we would like to focus on marriages and families as whole units and on the interaction of men, women and children in these social systems.

In the midst of loud laments for the once sacred inviolability of the family and general hand wringing over the increasing incidence of divorce and other signs of family breakdown, we seem to have forgotten the general drift of society away from older supports of our institutions. As we have become more industrialized and urbanized, as we have opened up more opportunities for full participation in education and occupations for people formerly restricted to narrow roles, we have seen changes in all our institutions. The old roles for men and women in marriage no longer "work" to support the stability of the structure. To continue to try to salvage a marriage on the basis of persons' fulfilling roles which are no longer meaningful seems to us to be clinging to a mythology which has already been shattered. We choose to view marriage as the potential structure in which individuals can interact so as to recognize and mutually support the ways that each member strives for gratification and self-actualization in an ever-changing society. If the members of the family want to establish a supportive recognition of each other, we consider that family viable.

Learned roles are not the only way our society structures our behavior. Many of our attitudes and "sets," and thus much of our behavior, have become habitual reactions, to the point of becoming unconscious, and it is this that we refer to as character. It is important to repeat here that character is not style. Character is that habitualness, comfortably ensconced in us, taught by our society and backed up by the weight of morality, that makes it right for us and, by extension, right for those in our community and in our society. Character can be seen as deviant when elements of the behavior are not acceptable to family or social class groups. Children who don't do well in school, make friends outside accepted eligibles, don't dress "right," don't make right religious decisions, may be seen as deviant. For their failure to internalize the value system, as well as for their lack of guilt or remorse, we refer to them as victims of "character disorders."

In the midst of the unconscious habitualness of character and the all-too-conscious pressures to fulfill our roles, there emerge dimensions of temperament which we refer to as style. Existing in each of us, style can be freely displayed, and thus recognized and supported by others, only by conscious identification and communication. But we fearfully resist exposing this style too openly even while we yearn to develop our own fulfillment. We see our heroes as somehow flung free of this constraint and having the courage to be themselves. "If I have to ask, it's not worth it." "If I have to ask, they will only support me because I made them do it." "If I have to ask, they might say no and turn their back on me." So we turn away from revealing our identity, turn away from the support that could be waiting for us, turn away from intimacy and the joy of being known for who we are.

We see the family, then, as a wonderful opportunity to be a mutually supportive primary group, a group wherein each member can ask for and receive the recognition of his individuality and the support for using his own style for the achievement of gratification. It is no longer an institution where certain roles are imposed to make one member the "head of household" and required "breadwinner" while the other serves as mother, helpmeet, housewife, regardless of the temperament style that might be dissonant with these required behaviors and the societal values that support them.

In the light of this discussion as to our orientation toward family structure and functioning, we approach this area of family counseling with our usual threefold system.

TEMPERAMENT STYLES IN HUSBAND-WIFE INTERACTION

Of first importance is the husband-wife relationship and the occurrence of family dissonance at this level. Although we see distinct male-female, husband-wife roles fading fast in today's family picture, we still encounter this as a basic problem in marital therapy. Because the changed picture, particularly of adult women's activities, represents a quite pervasive social change, we find the Withdrawers, with their reluctance to move into new situations, particularly affected. In fact, a large majority of the marriage problems which are brought to us involve a Withdrawer husband and a wife who has the temperament style cluster of the Doer or the Intenser.

The Withdrawer, more so than any other temperament style, is devoted to role. It fits with his need for regularity and, most importantly, reinforces his sense of what is right. This is, of course, what is familiar and customary, and this very "usualness" takes on a morality. "What's *wrong* with you? We never do it *that* way!" is the way the Withdrawer responds to any change in family routine. If things are not going "as usual," the Withdrawer experiences the panic of things being out of control. The Withdrawer husband in today's family has generally accepted the role prescription of head of household and may display his temperament by filling this role with worry, protection, guidance, and outright orders to the others in the family, meanwhile bemoaning their shortcomings.

A Doer wife in such a marriage may accept, or at least not be upset over, this behavior, particularly if she is busy with the high level of activity involved in mothering small children and being an active community contributor. In this way, she uses her temperament to do for others, but there is often a diminution of the need for her activity at home as her children grow. Doers may then suffer the depression of uselessness or, in a more healthy solution, begin to think of their own gratification. It is at this juncture, when the Doers turn to new interests, that the Withdrawer senses betrayal. Doers, knowing themselves as capable problem-solvers, often take on handling their spouses' feelings as well, and present themselves for therapy hoping to learn what they can do to change their husbands' responses. Doers have a hard time facing the fact that they cannot by their sheer activity alter the other person's temperamental reactivity.

Other temperament style clusters can also be dissonant with the roles and societal values which seem to be imposed upon them by marriage and family life. The Adapter man, often gentle, distractible, and somewhat passive in terms of not being assertive about his own point of view, but yielding to his perception of what will please others, finds the breadwinner role and the need to be a paragon of masculine responsibility a veritable straitjacket. He may find some relief in alcohol, drugs, or passive withdrawal—and find himself and his spouse embroiled in new problems.

Intenser women, having difficulty around the free expression of feelings, fail the self-effacing, mother/housewife role by appearing irrational, ineffective, and crazy to their less intense spouses. When such a couple comes for marital counseling, it is the woman's intense style that is seen, at least initially, as "the problem."

Intenser men tend to overinvest in their role of provider and are involved with their work world or other extra-familial activities. Often seen as socially acceptable wheeler-dealers, they are always overextending their available time and energy and family needs are seriously unmet. Their spouses may feel like nags attempting to eke out their share of their husbands' attention and time, and their relationships suffer from lack of reciprocal intimacy. The whole dissonant system is "no"—no recognition, no communication, no support, nothing.

TEMPERAMENT STYLES IN PARENT-CHILD INTERACTION

We rarely encounter a couple in marital counseling when there are not evident signs of distress also in parent-child relationships, if they have children. Parents are generally in the dominating position here. By the time we become parents, habitual reactions and our interpretation of the role of parents have become so hardened that we generally feel not only morally justified but obligated to mold our children according to the family myth that we have accepted. Parents, faced with our statement that their children come with their own temperament dimensions, will often despair about both the fate of their child and their own preconceived goals as parents.

In the NYLS one of the important findings was that parent-child dissonance resulted when the given temperament of the child was not recognized by parents. In nonrecognition of their child's temperament individuality, parents often worked against that temperament. The difficulty for the parent, of interacting with a child who did not provide gratifying closure for the parent's individual temperament sytle, was, of course, not the focus of the earlier work with children. But in our work we see all parties of an interaction as having temperament styles which become an important component in their interactive exchange.

Our work with couples and/or with families has been to promote the ideal of the recognition of everyone's style and to support each individual in using his style to strive for gratification and closure. This does not mean that each and every member can be supported at all times by every other family member. In fact, it seems to suggest that an individual can look to others outside the family enclave for such support. At adolescence the tendency is to move in this direction in order to achieve necessary growth. The attempt at this time to step up parental pressure towards conforming to family values often causes another rift of dissonance. Admitting each member's need for confirmation and support may make this period less traumatic for all. Accepting the givens of temperament in each individual means the eventual shift of family energy away from the maintenance of family myths and toward the emergence of each member's individuality through interaction.

WORKING WITH TEMPERAMENT IN FAMILY COUNSELING

We have carried out our family or marriage counseling in the same manner as our individual and group counseling. As a rule we see the couple or family together. After introducing our procedure and its validation, we start with individual recognition. It is interesting to see how much a spouse or others in the family have really been able to discern a style in the others. The additional observational evidence can make a recognition session spirited, as well as confirming. We can often begin to see just how much tractability remains in the relationship and if there is anything acceptable about the other person's style. It is usually very hard for a couple or a family to hear us say that we are not out to change any of them. This usually leads to a long discussion restating our acceptance of temperament persistence and our focus on dissonance. The counseling may never move beyond this point in some cases. The prospect of changing a "frog into a prince" or the "ugly duckling into a swan" may be too persuasive to let go of.

If the family members are willing to consider the acceptance of the individual dimension of each other, then communication for and recognition of the style cluster of each other are the next hurdle. Here we begin to meet resistance. The first resistance is simply to the self-exposure, carefully defended and obscured in the past. The second layer of resistance is the insistence that recognition should come spontaneously from the others; this has the peculiar intensity of an infantile demand. A third layer of resistance is simply the desire to not yet give up control or manipulation of others.

We feel that the key to our system is communication for support toward closure. Over and over we stress that individual fulfillment requires the interactive support of another. The universal protest is, "I should not be dependent." So often we refer to others who have "made it," never fully realizing the destructive unreality of that myth. The establishment of this mutual need for recognition and support becomes the royal road to consonance and success in marriage and family living.

NOTES ON FAMILY COUNSELING

Following are two examples from our clinical work with family counseling based on the application of temperament concepts. The R. family consisted of parents and two children, teenage and pre-teenage, so that all were able to participate in the process as an interactive group. In the second example, the one child in the family was too young for active participation in this type of counseling. We worked with the husband and wife, but incorporated the child into our view of this as an interactive family unit with three individual temperament styles to be taken into account.

Case Study: The R. Family

The R. family first came to our attention with the father, Sam, preparing the way in the course of seeking individual therapy for depression. The depression occurred at the time of a change of jobs within his company. This choice of us as therapists led him to examine himself in terms of temperament for the first time. After some initial therapy, he joined one of our groups. His depression seemed to clear rather quickly with group support. We assessed his style cluster as that of Withdrawer, and he seemed to benefit from acceptance of this identification.

About a year after he stopped attending group meetings, Sam called to make an appointment for himself and his wife to talk over some family problems. Their problems seemed to center with their styles of parenting, Sam viewing Helen as demanding and overorganizing, and Helen viewing Sam as yielding and overprotective. The decision was made to bring in the entire family, which included a teenage daughter and a pre-teenage son. The family had recently moved—within the same metropolitan area but away from the former neighborhood and school district.

We first proceeded to the temperament self-identity of each. Sam's wife, Helen, held an executive position in a large retail corporation and was decidedly a *Doer* who displayed a great deal of intensity in her heavy investment in her activities. She not only capably performed her own job, she also planned the family's activities, concerned herself with everyone's adequacy, and attempted to instill a kind of happy spirit she had known in her own family. She wanted very much to help others avoid unhappiness and offered numerous helpful hints to promote health and happiness. She accepted the identification of her style, but did not fully acknowledge the individuality of others and their assumption of responsibility for themselves.

Cathy was a "perfectionist" by family labeling, with a determination to do everything to the utmost that pervaded her entire life system. Her straight "A" school record, her hours of practicing for the swim team, her constant efforts to improve her performance, and her attention to minute counting of calories to maintain her ideal of a perfect weight were all family legends. These tendencies were spoken of by the parents with pride and admiration, but also with a certain rueful admission that her *Persistence* became difficult for them to live with.

Jeffy was seen as an *Adapter,* armed with the Adapter's technique of agreeableness. His indifferent performance and easy distractibility were a real trial to mother and sister and a worry to Sam, but he defended himself with a kind of bland innocence. He seemed to delight in everyone's anxieties about. him.

The family interaction had become involved in a struggle by each person to use his own temperament to manipulate others in the family. We tried during the family group meetings to help each realize what his own potential gratification might be and how to ask for support towards this closure.

Helen was able to concentrate more consistently on her work and other personal projects. She acknowledged her need for the family's support in these pursuits. As she received this support she diminished her intense and active interest and intervention in others' happiness and success. She was more realistic about what she could do for the family and there was not only more responsibility delegated but less bickering about outcomes.

Jeffy was given more responsibility to come to grips with school demands and was encouraged to work closer with his father, who could be more objective and encouraging than Helen and less distraught about the possibilities of failure. Sam became more of a focal point for family direction and interaction, and although still somewhat apprehensive, began to participate more in potentially gratifying and enjoyable activities. There was a greater sense of a clear direction and of mutual support between the two parents.

Cathy's difficulties grew as the rest of the family seemed to function better. She continued to fend off helpful intervention, attempting to intensify her perfectionistic, ritualistic behavior. Only slowly and gradually was she able to work out patterns of helpful interaction with her family and make some gains in closeness. We can foresee her need for further therapy in the stress of separation and growth into young adulthood.

Case Study: The N. Family

Jean and Terry N. were a young couple in their 30s, parents of a four-year-old girl. They came to us as the final step before repairing to the divorce court. Mrs. N. was pressing for divorce, but Mr. N. wanted to explore one more approach. He had become aware of our work with temperament and saw this as a possibly helpful approach.

When we met with them for the first time, Mrs. N.'s anger was obvious. She saw this meeting as a maneuver of her husband and apparently expected some heavy-handed manipulation from us. As is our wont, we introduced our operative concepts by giving notice that our goal was not to change anyone, nor did we think we could do that even if we wanted to. This produced an almost instantaneous, somewhat startled, diminution of her anger. We then began to discuss temperament and style and our concepts of their persistence in adults. There remained, however, a nagging uneasiness in Mrs. N.'s participation and this finally dissipated when we announced that, though we were willing to work on their relationship, our purpose was not to save their marriage. She greeted this statement with relief and told us that with that understanding she would be willing to undertake a specified number of joint sessions with her husband. We decided that 12 sessions would be enough to cover our threefold approach and this was agreed to with alacrity.

The next session was devoted to self-identification through scrutiny of the self-rating questionnaire. We found it both interesting and helpful to have each spouse carefully listen to and confirm or correct the other's self-impression. A dimension hidden to oneself can sometimes be seen by the spouse or the therapists. It is often around these areas of surprise that we find the greatest impetus to understanding and eventual use in interaction. Jean was clearly a Doer, having worked to help put Terry through school, even while having and rearing their child. She dealt with family problems and solutions. But more than this, there was an emerging intensity that could be appreciated by others but that she was not aware of displaying. This was noticeable as she talked: tensely drawn expression would give way to forced smiles while her eyes seemed to pop out. What we witnessed was the seeming contradiction of *intense inhibition*. When apprised of this, she acknowledged that she had been engaged in this suppressive behavior far back into her childhood, quite fearful of displaying any "loss of control." She was often restless with the low key of their marital life and yearned for outside stimulation, yet refused to push for more activity. Other observations showed her to have a low threshold of response, with a fairly high degree of persistence and non-distractibility. Her husband was often aware that something was bothering her when she came home, but she usually denied his inquiries—only later would she finally "blow-up." Control of intensity was a constant issue with her, especially around her child.

Terry, the son of a minister, had also trained for a life in the ministry, but did not pursue this after graduation from seminary. Terry's decision not to pursue this career was accomplished more by default than anything else. He had little "confidence" in himself and needed a good bit of bolstering, but deplored that need. He was rather low on the activity scale and at times it looked as if his eyelids were permanently set at half mast. He seemed to have a generally high quality of mood which was expressed with low intensity—producing, at times, a kind of suffocating smoothness. Despite all of this, he was quite likeable and agreeable, open to suggestion, but so adaptive and distractible that he might never be seen as being decisive. He easily perceived his wife's intensity, but felt uneasy about his capacity to do anything about it. Terry was most definitely an Adapter. He was most unhappy in accepting his high adaptability; for some reason this term took on pejorative overtones, as if to indicate overconformity. He wanted to be seen as resolutely independent, not needing direction from others, capable of being a man, as he saw it. In reality, he needed a good bit of feedback on his performance and could effectively utilize positive support. He needed to find out how things were done, but often held back, jeopardizing his job. He more or less felt his agreeable quality of mood would carry the day.

Their problem of interaction seemed to center around Jean's fearfulness of losing control (intensity) and Terry's denial of his need for helpful feedback (adaptability). We concentrated on helping Terry develop the communication for feedback and information from his boss and Jean. With Jean, we worked for the communication of her feelings to Terry as they occurred and the freer expression of her desires for activity (movies, plays, etc.). After surviving a period of some awkward attempts at the interaction, they eventually succeeded to the point where they felt that continuing the relationship was worthwhile.

Utilizing the parent questionnaire developed by the New York Longitudinal Study, we helped them to identify their daughter as quite active and intense. The confrontation of the two similar temperament styles had resulted in skirmishes between Jean and the child. Jean, in playing out the mother role, had seen her daughter as "headstrong" and "hard to handle." In her need to take charge, she was apparently oblivious that she had a daughter who also wanted to take charge. Jean had felt angry that Terry, in his adaptive way, got along amicably with the girl and felt no need to make a big issue out of behavior that Jean found highly annoying. Once the identification was made, Jean was able to relax her tight control of the situation and Terry was able to better understand and help mediate in this mother/daughter dissonance. Their daughter, given acceptance of her temperament as a highly active and intense person, was now asked how she wanted to do things and afforded help if she needed it.

In checking up, some months after therapy was discontinued, we found that this family had been able to maintain the more open communication of temperament needs to one another. Both husband and wife had been able to extend this freer communication in their careers. Jean had been recognized for her efficiency and intense involvement by a promotion. Terry was more at ease in asking for support from his supervisor. As they received more closure for their individual temperaments, the tension in the marriage lessened. We believe the mutual recognition and support of their individual styles will enable them to continue a marriage that was headed for dissolution.

Part V

A Look to the Future

14

Further Applications of Temperament Counseling

We have extended the uses of our work with styles and their interactions to essentially non-therapeutic areas. Three areas in which we have made some tentative explorations are: 1) child placement agencies; 2) educational institutions; and 3) occupational settings.

TEMPERAMENT APPLICATION IN CHILD PLACEMENT AGENCIES

Child placement involves the interaction of foster parents or adoptive parents and their children. As consultants to placing-out and adoptive agencies over a period of thirty years, we have become increasingly aware that the "failures" in placement are often due to dissonance between the new parents' temperaments and the placed child's temperament. We are not implying that we can ignore the effect of a disturbed past in the life of the placed child, but we think that a long-neglected area has been the fit of the temperament dimensions of the parent with the temperament of the child. Foster parents particularly see themselves as influentially bringing a new (and better) way of life to foster children. They are often so committed in this work that their personal sense of success or failure hinges on the outcome. Once dissonance asserts its presence, the usual foster parent response is to further emphasize their own temperament

179

dimensions and finally to ask for replacement of the child when this does not produce change. Sadly, it is the child who is left with the burden of failure: "Something wrong with him," "Can't overcome bad upbringing," etc.

Foster parents who are Doers often seem to have the most dissonance, followed closely by the Intensers. Doers think that the same mastery activity they expend on a work project will effectively carry over to human relationships. Thus, they feel obligated, no, duty-bound, to approach the child by problem solving for him and often taking over and finishing things for him. This behavior might fit in with an adaptive child, but certainly not with a child who is also a Doer. Such a child experiences the dissonance of his closure being constantly frustrated. His eventual response is to object *loudly*, have temper tantrums, and generally not act appropriately grateful for what is being done for him. Although the expression of such dissonance may be somewhat delayed, when it becomes actively expressed this dissonance may bring on requests for removal of the child. Adapter children are often infantilized by Doer parents who anticipate and solve problems for them. Dissonance then appears in school where teachers have a student not ready or willing to enter the learning process. It is difficult to get these foster parents to discipline consistently because they tend to be overprotective and to feel that teachers do not understand the child's problems.

Intenser foster parents think of themselves as the fountain of energy. They are particularly defeated by Adapters (who have low intensity and are non-assertive), often feeling that they are being taken advantage of. The tremendous investment of energy eventually drains the Intenser and we are called to "come get this kid before we go crazy or murder him." Intenser foster parents also run afoul of Intenser children who often engage them in displays of counter-intensity. Again, after bleeding most of their energy, the foster parents call for removal.

Caseworkers rightfully complain that the types of foster parents described above do not listen to pre-placement advice, nor do they seek help during placement. There is no way they can be successful parents in the situations noted without some knowledge of temperament and their own self-identification. Without this awareness, they fear that dissonance may reflect their own failure to be effective parents.

We believe that adoptive parents run into the same tangle of problems. Of course, there may initially be a higher level of commitment than in foster parents, but the effect of this may simply be to produce more determination to succeed as an influencing parent. Dissonance may be experienced much more keenly by adoptive parents than by natural parents since they feel somewhat estranged from the inherent temperament of the child. It is almost essential that an adopted child be experienced as quick to adapt if there is to be some acceptable intimacy and identification. The greater need for psychiatric services for adopted children may stem from the disturbing pressure of dissonance. We think it may be especially beneficial for adoptive parents to be aware of their own style clusters as well as to obtain as early data as possible about the temperament of their child.

Training for Temperament Counseling

It is quite feasible to teach temperament identification and counseling to child placement agency personnel. We have given a number of workshops for social workers in such agencies and the concept is quickly grasped. In groups, social workers easily identify their own temperament and feed back identifying information to each other.

We think that a longer period of training would be productive. Even though there is a quick grasp of the concept of and actual recognition of dimensions of temperament, there remains the problem of how to use this in helpful interaction. Social workers, used to thinking in more traditional psychodynamic terms, can then begin seeing the dynamic interaction around temperament dissonance, the defensive uses of hypertrophy, and the style-appropriate ways of gaining closure by asking for recognition and confirmation. Recognizing the temperaments of others, either of children or other adults, is an important part of the training. If foster parents and adoptive parents are given this help by trained social workers, we feel that real progress can be made in cutting down parent-child dissonance with its consequent emotional distress.

TEMPERAMENT IN EDUCATION

A further area for the application of temperament theory is in the educational field. Just as parents in the New York Longitudinal Study were counseled to reduce parent-child dissonance by the recognition and acceptance of their child's temperament, we have seen that teachers can help reduce problems in learning at school by this same recognition and acceptance of the various styles of the children in their classrooms. The educational experience which takes their individuality into account will enable most children to make satisfactory progress *at their own pace.* In discussions with teachers, we have found that they readily recognize temperament styles, e.g., the Slow-To-Warm-Up child or the Difficult child, and are familiar with the problems that ensue when all children are expected to fit into a standardized educational program. We find that teachers are also quick to recognize their own particular temperament styles and to acknowledge that their particular way of teaching and their expectations as to how their students will learn are greatly influenced by this style.

The factor of temperament individuality is obviously a significant one in the educational system. However, the protests of teachers, that most of today's public school classrooms are too large for such individual consideration, are well taken. And many teachers and parents want to concentrate educational efforts on the teaching of basics. Yet the fundamental goals of better class management and better "basic learning" may be served most efficiently by recognition that individual temperament differences affect learning.

Of interest, too, are the new regulations covering special education because it is here that we find special attention being paid to individual educational programming for each child in special education districts. Even more innovative here is the requirement that parents participate in the individual educational planning for their child. We can envision that parents who had been made cognizant of the importance of temperament in the developmental phases of children, and who had identified the temperament style of their particular child, could bring this special knowledge about their child to the individual educational planning sessions with the child's teacher. We think it is especially important for parents of learning disabled children to be aware of the factor of dissonance in parent-child, or even teacher-child, interaction. This may be playing a large part in determining the children's attitudes toward learning. The field of special education has approached the problems of educating children "where they are"—that is, taking into account the individual capabilities of children and helping them to utilize their individual strengths. In this way, this part of the educational field has been in the vanguard of new ideas in education and has set new objectives for the more conventional educational field to consider. The idea of considering the individual temperament of the child and the interaction between the child and his adult teachers as a part of the programming of the child's education seems very much in line with these objectives.

In working with teachers in workshops, we have tried to develop with their help an understanding of some of the classroom behavior of the children as being expressions of temperament styles. Since problems with particular children are usually uppermost in the minds of the teachers, they quickly respond to descriptions of some of the temperamental manifestations that are not in conformity with the expectations for a smooth-running class. For example, a child who has a high level of persistence will not respond quickly to a change in activity once he is involved in a task. The instruction to turn attention to another activity, usually welcomed by most of the children, may be ignored by the persistent child and if he is more pointedly approached, angry resistance may become evident. In some classrooms this can, of course, quickly become a pitched battle of wills, with resultant counseling attention for this "difficult child." The child who withdraws or is slow-to-adapt may also exhibit some resistance to changes in schedules or to new situations and will respond at a generally slower pace. The child who has a high approach temperament and is distractible may seem constantly on the move and has difficulty staying with a task to completion. For example, one teacher told of a girl who seemed to want to get into every activity that others were doing. The objective in her school, to have children working on different activities suitable to their capabilities, presented her with more stimulation than she could easily handle.

Her teacher said, "I know she is just trying to get attention by this behavior, and I try to give her extra attention . . ." When we suggested that perhaps the perceived motivation (to get attention) might be a projection of the teacher's own understanding of this behavior and might be held in abeyance while we simply looked at the behavior as reflecting the girl's temperament, she was able to think of this as simply this girl's way of responding in an environment where lots of stimulation was present.

Teachers, as well as parents, are often able to construct different interaction with children when they recognize and accept temperament as a given individual style of behavior. If the teacher is constantly trying to understand the *reasons* (i.e. motivations, subconscious or intentional) for the behavior of the child, she may attach a multitude of *meanings* that are not necessarily accurate. "She is trying to get attention," "He is stubborn," "She is so *good,*" may be the basis for the teacher's response to that child but may not be an accurate recognition of that child's temperament. We have learned that teachers can respond with recognition and acceptance when they have become aware of the temperament component in the behavior of their students. "I realize that you do not like to be interrupted while you are working, Johnny. You may work without interruption after recess period," is quite a different response from a firm insistence on conforming behavior and possibly a note to parents or the school counselor regarding Johnny's inability or refusal to follow instructions.

Of course, the important other side of the interactive process is identification and acceptance of the individual temperament style of the teacher himself. The expectations that we have of our own ways of behaving remain largely covert and inaccessible until we have brought them to consciousness and have decided to accept our individuality. Once teachers have learned to get in touch with their styles, they can think of their need to communicate this to others for recognition and support. Since the major part of the teacher's day is spent with children who are not perhaps sufficiently able to play a directly supportive role, the teacher may have a special need for communication opportunities with colleagues and supervisors. It may appear that this adds a new burden, that of learning to recognize and communicate temperament identification, to the heavy load the teacher already carries. However, it is likely that this would be a way to lighten the burden of good teaching and help repair and restore a sense of gratification to a job that is often draining and lacking in personal recognition.

TEMPERAMENT IN OCCUPATIONAL SETTINGS

In our therapy groups and with individual patients, we are often involved in discussions about interactions at work. Since most adults spend a large part of their lives in work settings, to imagine that interactions at this level are not affected by individual temperament differences is surely unrealistic. Yet there seems to be a consensus that temperament is best kept hidden in the occupational world, that there is no place for individual styles to be considered, and that the "real" world of business is concerned only with production figures, cost analysis, and the "bottom line" of profit. We are not sure that this is true, yet we have heard comments from our patients that policies of many companies do not permit consideration of the individuality of their employees. One wonders at the practice of underwriting health insurance, including psychiatric treatment, while failing to recognize that workers are individuals who bring their individual styles into their work life and who will suffer from the stresses of dissonance if they try to carry out a work life where fulfillment or gratification is not possible.

There have been countless books attempting to define the internal strategies of management in our large businesses. Ways of managing have been described and certain types of persons and their "styles" of executive behavior have been discussed. Yet we have not seen an emphasis on the interactive exchange between management and workers for the purpose of establishing conditions for maximizing satisfaction in the performance of the job; nor have we seen any description of real communication between those at the management level for recognition, support and repair. This is not only a higher-level executive problem, but a problem for the assembly line worker as well. In most work situations there appears to be little communication of this nature, although corporations have become aware in recent years of the importance of "communication" at all levels. However, the "communications skills training" that has become commonplace in most large corporations has remained somewhat at the level of "effectiveness" in expediting the productive goals of the company, rather than in increasing the level of the employee's satisfaction with his work. We still find that the prevailing idea is that need for support and recognition is a sign of weakness and must be withheld from communication to co-workers or to those above or below one's position on the occupational ladder.

It is apparent that each temperament style will show a predictable reaction to certain work situations and each will feel a certain stress under certain conditions. Many of the case histories in earlier chapters show some of the interactive needs of various temperament styles and how dissonance can arise in the work situation when temperament style is not recognized and needs for satisfaction are not communicated. While there is still a lack of research on applications of temperament counseling in the occupational field, the effects seen among therapy patients of the lack of consonance in their involvement with the occupational world indicate the need for such counseling.

PROSPECTS IN PREVENTION

Several times in this book we have referred to social changes which have made the emergence of individual uniqueness possible. Changing work roles and the breaking down of racial and sexual stereotypes have gone a long way toward reducing the rigidity of role-defined behavior. Scientific and knowledge explosions have largely demythologized our lives so that we are no longer hemmed in by inappropriate structures. Our reactions to the devastating results of authoritarian power structures, especially to the Nazi holocaust and to revelations of political corruptions have blunted our willingness to conform unquestioningly to the authority of the state and its leaders.

In a society where older norms of behavior seem no longer appropriate and older societal values, underwritten by institutionalized morality, no longer compelling, we see an increasing incidence of the confusion and depression at the individual level that reflect the normlessness of the society at large. For many, the search for a preventive approach to mental illness is the search for a "road back" to a more stable society, perhaps supported by strengthened institutions in the hands of powerful authorities. However, the prospect of freedom of the individual to function in a way that allows for his self development, while interacting with others for whom a similar goal is entertained, seems to be a preferable way to work towards the prevention of emotional distress.

A review of the Thomas, Chess and Birch book, *Temperament and Behavior Disorders in Children* concluded with this paragraph:

> A book like this cries out for replicative study. It holds tremendous promise in the field of *preventative psychiatry*. The possibility of useful anterolongitudinal studies of all children is exciting. Most of all, by accommodating development to the child's unique temperament we may be taking a long step toward the contemporary goal of responsible individual freedom (1).

Now, 10 years later, after extrapolating and extending the NYLS findings to adults, we are more enthusiastic than ever about the possibilities of a truly preventative approach. The therapeutic uses of temperament, as fruitful as they have been, emphasize the importance of the early development of consonance in parent-child relationships, and later in the growing emergence of our unique style as adults.

Since the ability of the individual to go through stages of growth and development occurs in the family primary group, and since marriage and family groups continue throughout our lives to be an essential primary group for the great majority of us, we see the marital dyad and the parent-child interaction as extremely important focal points for the introduction of temperament counseling.

When viewed from the point of view of style, marriage and subsequent parenthood seem often to be carried on in a climate of conflict of styles. This dissonance is further reinforced by our individual insistence that our style will prevail, will finally be seen as the dominant sensible view. In marriage this may be experienced very early in the relationship, or only after years of continued adaptation. The net effect of the ubiquitous presence of dissonance, early or late, is to establish marriage as a relationship grounded in struggle. Most of the current attempts to correct marital discord are concerned with working out more effective strategies in dealing with struggle. In this struggle, unfortunately, the "confirmation" of our style is fostered through its direct or indirect imposition on another. It is true that, in the past, roles and societal values have attempted to structure marital interaction, but these seem to have been stripped away. We question the viability of counseling which proposes new ways to contain old dissonances. Symptomatic responses and emotional distress, of one degree or another, are seen by us as largely emanating from the chronic effects of dissonance.

Maintaining a dissonant relationship demands that crucial elements of one's style cluster be denied and largely unrecognized. However, these components cannot be unrecognized forever. Even as an Adapter is smilingly adapting to the outrageous demands of another, he is aware (or becoming aware) that there is a limit to what his adaptability can accept. The Intenser, while straining to satisfy everyone's feelings, becomes aware of the need for gratifying recognition of his intensity. The breaking through of a heretofore hidden element of one's style is often experienced as distressing, not only in respect to the outer world's expectations but also to the habitual system that we identify as our self. The external and internal warfare that ensues creates eventually a symptomatic picture of this struggle.

We see our patients caught in this struggle to individuate themselves. We find almost instant relief in their symptomatic picture when we help them to identify their *self* as containing their dimensions of temperament apparently at war within them and with the world around them. They no longer have to change themselves. It is now more a matter of fully being themselves and communicating this self-being to others around them for significant confirmation. We think of this as the interactive component of individuality—a confirmed knowing of us that is especially important for closure and fulfillment.

When dealing with dissonant marriages, we proceed from individual style cluster identity to the interactive communications. If interactive communication can bring no confirmatory response, we recognize the dissonance as unbridgeable and do not see any use in further counseling toward reestablishment of the marriage. Our experiences in marriage counseling give us little hope for correcting years of dissonance.

We have mentioned the difficulties in resolving dissonance in marriage to underscore our belief that a preventive approach utilizing temperament theory would probably best be carried out with premarital counseling. Such counseling could consist first of all of the identification of style clusters of each party. We could then proceed to models of communication for confirmation and repair. In the course of the counseling, we could approach the manifestations of dissonance. If the dissonance is based on a consistent demand that the other change elements of his or her style, then we would strongly advise against the marriage. Any attempt to dispel the dissonance by adapting would also be seen as not leading to future fulfillment.

We would encourage such a counseled couple to "check in" for current temperament assessment periodically. Most important would be the establishment of prenatal contact, if they are becoming parents, for the purpose of preparing for recognition of temperament manifestations early in the life of the infant. It is hoped that with the background of parental consonance there will be a natural flow of consonance in the parent-child relationship. Again, this could be checked on and followed through the years of child development. We conceive of a child, in consonant interaction with parents, fully aware of his style and capable of communicating this in various interactions with others for their confirmation and support. This would lead not only to a conscious early self-identification, but, just as importantly, to a capacity to identify another's style.

We can appreciate the utopian nature of this ideal of prevention. It is as yet largely untested, but we see no overriding objection to carrying the pioneer work of Thomas and Chess to such possible fruition. In our era marked by alienation, depersonalization, and dehumanization, it suggests an approach that restores our individuality back to our beginnings and broaches the possibility of an interaction toward mutual closure and fulfillment instead of an unceasing cycle of struggle and manipulation.

REFERENCE

1. RUBENSTEIN, M. Book review of Thomas, A., Chess, S., and Birch, H. G. *Temperament and Behavior Disorders in Children.* New York: New York University Press, 1968, in *Child Welfare*, XLVIII, 10, December, 1969, p. 627.

15

Toward a Psychology of How

The development of new ideas is never sudden and unique but occurs in a climate of thinking that is supportive of the new concept. Much as we tend to give credit to Darwin for the concept of evolution and to Freud for his theories on the unconscious factor of behavior, these ideas themselves occurred in an intellectual setting which was anticipating such a development.

From antiquity, two views of the basis of behavior have appeared, now one, now the other gaining ascendency. One view appeared to suggest that behavior was constructed from within. Hippocrates identified four humors and gave them names—choleric, phlegmatic, sanguine, and bilious—after the supposed connection to bodily fluids, suggesting that such states were persistent and predictive of ways of thinking and acting. The idea that body structure carries with it a tendency to act in predictable ways is often found in literature and in folk wisdom. ("*Let me have men about me that are fat; Sleek-headed men and such as sleep o'nights: Yond Cassius has a lean and hungry look; He thinks too much: such men are dangerous,*" Julius Caesar, Act 1, Scene 2.) On the other hand, the view that behavior, particularly pathological or unacceptable behavior, comes from outside the individual, from an external agent which invades the person, also recurs. Up until recently there has been a view that

191

psychopathological behavior occurred because the devil, or dybbuk, or such like, had entered the person, was possessing and driving him crazy. In a sense, even presently there is a view of psychopathology which strongly suggests that the external causative agent has been wrong thinking or inept parents whose effect must be rooted out and exorcised before healthy functioning can take place.

In the development of the sciences of social behavior, any ideas of given states, instincts, or constitutional predispositions have tended to be discounted since they seem to imply the workings of an inexorable fate or a mystical destiny, evidence of a more primitive metaphysical thinking. At the same time, the supposition of possession or control by an external agent (including parents) whose machinations must remain covert cannot become the subject of objective scientific investigation.

Yet, the concern for knowing the psychodynamics of mental functioning and social behavior continues to intrigue us, not only in terms of understanding pathological behavior but in terms of understanding "normal" mental processes and social functioning.

A persistent theme in the study of human behavior has been the search for meaning. *Why* do people behave as they do? We have always attempted to search out the reasons, the causes, that underlie behavior. Freudian psychology enjoyed much popular acceptance because it offered *deeper* and more novel reasons for the underlying causes of human behavior. His view that reason for behavior had become, for the most part, irretrievably repressed into the unconscious, where a battle for control was being waged between libidinous drives and restrictive external demands, gave us one answer to our persistent *why*.

But for another school of behavioral scientists the conjectures of psychoanalysis could only remain conjectures and thus unavailable for scientific investigation. Their search for meaning turned to the more overt and observable *content* of behavior. Behavior then was to be studied in terms of *what* was emitted and, of course, their view came to the conclusion that behavior was the result of what sort of stimulus was presented. For the behaviorism school of thought, behavior is whatever we condition and reinforce it to be. In this view the individual can be seen as largely undifferentiated in terms of what the content of his behavior will be: a receiver who will become an individual in terms of his responses to his unique set of environmental influences.

In the last two decades we have been witnessing a shift of thinking, appearing particularly in the literature on child development, away from the position of the behaviorists. Publications have been coming out in increasing numbers which attest to the fact that students of child development believe the newborn infant, even the fetus in utero, is an individual participating in behavior and is a part of interactive relationships. No longer seen as an organism to whom the environment is simply a huge chaotic confusion, the infant has been observed to act and react in a coherent and meaningful way with this environment.

Currently the work of Edward Wilson (1) and others has turned the attention of many social behavioral scientists, as well as the biological scientists, to the subject of sociobiology: the idea that our genetic make-up and the push of genes toward survival determines much social behavior. Such a view again challenges the theories of behavior which see the individual as a blank page upon which the social environment writes a program of behavior, or upon which the experiences of life will cause certain action to be expressed and other actions to be repressed or extinguished. As sociobiologist Robert Trivers points out, such a theory must embrace the idea that, "The child is not just an empty vessel to be filled by parents, but a sophisticated organism" (2).

It is in this intellectual "climate," in which human behavior is seen as more than imposed upon the individual by his environment and his "conditioning," that the work of the NYLS directed by Thomas and Chess can be appreciated. It is not to deny the impact of social experiences of the individual but to include the evidence of the presence of inherent temperamental dimensions in the study of individual behavior that this study has turned its attention. In this study we are provided with convincing evidence of the presence of identifiable temperament dimensions and individual variations at early, pre-language stages in life.

Our present work, by extrapolating these concepts to adults, seeks to take evidence of temperament into account in studying interactive behavior throughout life, rather than thinking of it in terms of earlier developmental stages only. Like the directors of the work with children, it is not our intention to foster a deterministic position in any controversy of inherent versus environmental factors in human behavior. Our position is rather one of synthesis or of systemic thinking which allows for many components and tries to emphasize the interaction of these components. In bringing attention to the dimensions, still rather unrigorously defined and tested, of temperament in adults, we do not wish to challenge or dispute the importance of the cognitive or the physical growth of the individual on his behavior, nor do we by any means wish to ignore the contributions to knowledge about human personality and behavior made by psychoanalytic, behavioristic, or symbolic interactionist thinking. We do wish to make a case for the extension of concepts of temperament into the adult years and to show that it is a basis upon which interactive behavior is played out throughout life stages.

Our speculation is that before the "why" of motivation, before the "what" of conditioning, there is a primary state, a given set of responses and actions whose effect on behavior is in the realm of "how." How we go about doing, feeling, thinking, relating. Our *style* of behavior is something we are born with. It is now possible to think of individualism as born, rather than individualism as imposed or acquired.

Our point of view accepts temperament givens and the behavioral manifestation of those givens without reference to "why" and "what." In fact, we feel that the preoccupation with the "whys" and the "whats" has been instrumental in distorting and even extinguishing the dimensions of "how" so that many of us have no consciousness of how we are being who we are and have settled into habitual reactions. Staying within the confines of psychology as a scientific discipline which observes behavior, the concept of temperament enables us to observe *how* behavior is displayed, *how* an individual responds in interaction, *how* an individual manifests developmental stages. We need not think of his behavior as something theoretically molded and shaped by a powerful environment which may have become a part of his "unconscious." Instead we are talking about the establishment of consciousness of what is displayed and observable.

From this framework of observing the openly displayed ways in which individuals present themselves, recorded throughout this book, we believe that a psychology that starts with the question of *how* an individual behaves contributes to understanding interactive behavior. It is *how* we display ourselves that confronts those who interact with us, and by means of which we can establish consonant or dissonant social relationships. It is *how* we present ourselves that is met with the gratification that is sensed as closure, or the unacceptance that leaves us with unmet drives which push for the now elusive satisfaction in distorted and unproductive ways.

A psychology of *how* turns us quite consciously toward our self— our self-acceptance, our self-history. How gives us an overview of our life and a recognition of the way things are and have been. As we look back on our life we see the emergence of a stylistic pattern by which we organize our cognitive experience, meet new developmental happenings and establish new existential ground for ourselves. It is essentially a way of educating ourselves in our selves, a way of knowing us—and hopefully knowing others.

Many mysteries remain, but we can now begin to face the conundrum of human behavior with a new view of *who* we are—*how* we are—and no longer restrict ourselves to questions of *why* or *what* we are.

REFERENCES

1. WILSON E. O. *On Human Nature*. Cambridge: Harvard University Press, 1978.
2. TRIVERS, R., quoted in *Time Magazine*, August 1, 1977, p. 57.

Appendices

Appendix A

Temperamental Characteristics

1. *Activity Level*

The person whose activity level is high will be physically energetic, usually enjoying and preferring active participation. If you would rather play in a group than be an audience, or climb a mountain rather than enjoy the view, or if you often see life and relationships as presenting problems about which you want to *do* something, you may be a person who ranks high on the scale of activity. Newborns display this temperamental reactivity by lying quietly and appearing fairly placid if *low,* or by squirming, kicking, engaging in a great deal of movement if *high.* Try to locate yourself on the scale by thinking whether you tend more toward low activity or high activity.

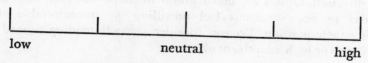

low   neutral   high

2. *Rhythmicity*

This refers to the usual way in which you function bodily. Do you wake at approximately the same time every morning, like to eat at the "right" time rather than "eat when you're hungry," like to see things carried out just right? In other words, do you regard yourself as usually *regular* in your daily patterns (the *high* end of the scale), or do you consider your-

199

self naturally *irregular* (and somewhat constrained by demands for routinized patterns) (the *low* end of the scale)?

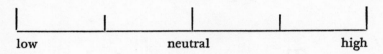

low   neutral   high

3. *Approach or Withdrawal*

When new situations or unexpected developments present themselves, do you find yourself somewhat reluctant, fearful, or, at least, uncomfortable, preferring, if you had the choice, to avoid these circumstances as much as possible? Or do you particularly like new situations and sense yourself as very "ready to do" with whatever situation may present itself. Children with withdrawal temperaments often cry when introduced to new foods, new people or new situations. If they are "approach" types, their parents often describe them as "never meets a stranger," or "at home wherever we take him." Try to locate yourself on the scale below as to how you react to new situations (*low* for withdrawal type, *high* for approach type).

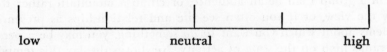

low   neutral   high

4. *Adaptiveness*

Some people readily adapt to changes and shift their behavior to comply with the expectations of others when the group needs to move in a new direction. Others are much slower to adapt and even after many exposures to new situations feel unwilling or uncomfortable about changing their position. Do you consider yourself tending toward low adaptiveness or high adaptiveness?

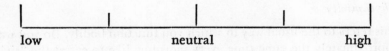

low   neutral   high

5. *Intensity*

Low intensity people are generally fairly deliberate in their actions and do not usually express themselves in superlatives. High intensity people feel very strongly about their environment and, if not actually verbal in expressing this, sometimes communicate it in intense gestures or even in an obvious effort to *repress* expressing it. Do you consider yourself tending toward low intensity or high intensity?

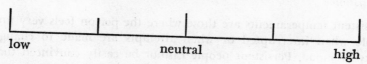

low   neutral   high

6. *Threshold of Responsiveness*

People with high thresholds seem not to become aware of sensory stimuli until they have become quite insistent. If you are very "sensitive" or aware of smells, temperatures, or noises, or pick up quickly on cues from others, you have a low threshold of responsiveness.

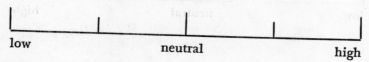

low   neutral   high

7. *Quality of Mood*

If you tend to respond to your surroundings in generally optimistic and rather uncritical enjoyment, you may be "global" or all-accepting in terms of your mood. You are at the *low* end of the continuum if you are generally more guarded and cautious in the situations which you select to enjoy.

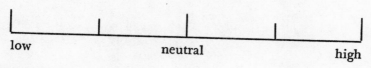

low   neutral   high

8. *Distractibility*

When engaged in an activity, do you find yourself easily turning to some other thoughts or activity? Or do you think you tend to stay with an activity and resist other competing stimuli? The distractible child, asked to come straight home from school, will be discovered to have stopped to watch a building construction, gotten into a ball game, gone into a friend's house, etc., etc. How do you think of yourself in this regard, *low* in distractibility or *high*?

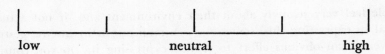

low   neutral   high

9. Persistence

Persistent temperaments are those where the person feels very uncomfortable when interrupted or when attempts are made to change an activity or mood. Persistent people cannot be easily convinced that an alternative activity should be undertaken. With children, we frequently think of persistence as "stubborn." Do you remember yourself as a "stubborn" child (*high* on the persistence scale), or does that description not seem to fit you as a usual way of reacting (*low* on the scale).

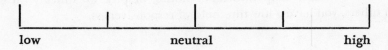

low   neutral   high

Appendix B

Style Clusters

The work with children by Thomas and Chess described three different constellations of temperament (sets of temperament dimensions that occurred together and described a typical style of behavior):

1. *Easy Children*—These children were regular or predictable, quick to adapt to new demands, had a generally positive quality of mood and only mild to moderate intensity. They comprised about 40 percent of the sample.

2. *Difficult Children*—These children were unpredictable, tended to withdraw from new situations, were non-adaptive, showed high intensity, and had a fairly low, discontented mood. There were only about 10 percent of the children in this group, but they produced a large proportion of the children who developed emotional distress.

3. *Slow-To-Warm-Up Children*—These children were also withdrawers and were slow to adapt, but had less intensity and more predictability than the Difficult Children. Approximately 15 percent of the sample were Slow-To-Warm-Up.

In our clinical work with adults, we have identified six different style clusters. We are not ready to speak in terms of how they are distributed. In any case, it is well to remember that in therapy situations we doubtless have a biased sample. We have used the name of the most salient temperament dimensions to identify each style cluster.

Our clinical findings in therapy groups:

1. *Persister* (*like Difficult Child*)—persistent, non-adaptive, low quality of mood, sometimes distractible. The Persister over-uses this trait. He holds the floor or holds you in conversation. He cannot be easily interrupted. He sees the world as attempting to silence him, thwart him. Typical Statements: "No one will listen to me." "I had not yet made the point I wanted to." "I don't have any friends!"

2. *Withdrawer*—withdrawal, low quality of mood, middle to low intensity, regular rhythmicity, and slow to adapt. The Withdrawer experiences new situations with some anxiety and raises many conditions and doubts before he can move ahead. Experienced as "controlling" and manipulative. Feels better when activity is successfully underway. Typical statements: "You haven't looked at all the things that can go wrong." "I probably won't like the (movie, play, new job, new location, etc.)." "He thinks I should be ready whenever he is."

3. *Intenser*—high intensity, low threshold, moderate to high persistence, mood expressed both positively and negatively. They *dramatize* and *emphasize* their reactions with words, body language, tone and rate of speech. (Sometimes intensity shows by marked "holding in.") Typical statements: "I'm *totally* exhausted." "She *hates* me." "It was a beautiful or (nauseating) day."

4. *Approacher*—high approach, high adaptive, low threshold of response, low activity, tendency toward distractibility. The Approachers appear to be waiting for stimulation from others. Thus, they can be exploited and "used" by others. They learn by integrating the experiences that others bring to them. Typical statements: "Sure I'll go—where are we going?" "I don't like being alone." "What should we do tonight?"

5. *Adapter*—low activity, high quality of mood, low threshold of response, high distractibility, high adaptability. The Adapter uses his adaptability to relate to others but his distractibility and global enjoyment do not keep him totally hooked to others. He often goes along outwardly but lives a private Walter Mitty life of his own. Typical statements: "Whatever you say, dear." "I *meant* to come, I just forgot." "I love you, too (said absently)." "Oh well, what *I* want to do isn't all that important."

6. *Doer*—high active, generally positive quality of mood, high intensity, middle level adaptiveness. He finds out where he likes the furniture by moving it around till he decides. If she is a homemaker, she has a houseful of macramé, a kitchen full of cooking, and is on the phone about one of her numerous committees. Typical statements: "Let's make an outline of what needs to be done." "We'll never know until we try it." "Do it now."

Index